GIVE ME WINGS

HOW A CHOIR OF FORMER SLAVES TOOK ON THE WORLD

Kathy Lowinger

annick press
toronto + new york + vancouver

© 2015 Kathy Lowinger (text)
Edited by Gena K. Gorrell
Designed by Sheryl Shapiro

Annick Press Ltd.

We acknowledge the support of the Canada Council for the Arts, the Ontario Arts Council, and the Government of Canada through the Canada Book Fund (CBF) for our publishing activities.

ONTARIO ARTS COUNCIL
CONSEIL DES ARTS DE L'ONTARIO
an Ontario government agency
un organisme du gouvernement de l'Ontario

Cataloging in Publication

Lowinger, Kathy, author
    Give me wings : how a choir of former slaves took on the world
/ by Kathy Lowinger.

Issued in print and electronic formats.
ISBN 978-1-55451-747-3 (bound).—ISBN 978-1-55451-746-6 (pbk.).—
ISBN 978-1-55451-748-0 (html).—ISBN 978-1-55451-749-7 (pdf)

    1. Jubilee Singers. 2. African American musicians—Biography—
Juvenile literature. I. Title.

ML28.N25J92 2015   j782.42162'9607300922   C2015-900394-6
                                                  C2015-900395-4

Published in the U.S.A. by Annick Press (U.S.) Ltd.

Printed in China

Visit us at: www.annickpress.com

Also available in e-book format. Please visit www.annickpress.com/ebooks.html for more details.
Or scan

In memory of my parents, Martha and Ernest Lowinger,
and for Alan and James Harnum

CONTENTS

ELLA SHEPPARD.

Photographed by BLACK.   Page 40

INTRODUCTION

*E*lla Sheppard was born a slave in 1851, in the southern state of Tennessee. She could expect a life of hard labor serving the people who owned her. Instead, she became a teacher, a musician, and an international celebrity. This book tells the story of how she did it.

The 1800s were a time of great suffering for black people in the United States. For the first sixty-odd years, most were still enslaved in the southern states, even after slavery was abolished in other states and other countries. From 1861 to 1865, the nation was torn apart by a bitter civil war that divided families, ravaged cities and farmland, and left over half a million people dead or disabled. Although slavery was abolished by the end of the war, most ex-slaves had to build their new lives with no jobs, no land, no belongings, and no education.

Ella Sheppard was lucky to enrol at Fisk University, but the school was about to close for lack of money. She and nine other teenaged ex-slaves set out to raise funds to keep the school open. It was far more difficult than they expected, yet they succeeded beyond their wildest imaginings. How did they do it? With music: spirituals and songs from their years of slavery. The songs they sang helped break down barriers between blacks and whites, and those same songs served as important roots for today's music: rock, pop, the blues, jazz, and hip-hop. Their music still says a lot to us today. The story of their courage and determination says even more.

Note that I have not described people of color as "African-American" because in those days, they were barely considered American at all. They were called Negro or colored or black, or many demeaning names. Of those terms, "black" is the most common today, and it is the term I use. Note also that all the quotes from Ella come directly from her diaries or letters.

Chapter 1

"NEVER A SLAVE!"

"My baby," Sarah told her mistress simply, "will never be a slave!"
— *a quote from Sarah Hannah Sheppard, Ella's mother*

Ella was only a scrap of a girl, far too young to be a spy. But that's what her mistress was asking her to be. Ella traced the rose pattern in the parlor carpet with her bare toe as Mistress Phereby's voice rose and fell.

"Your ma is a house slave, and there's no knowing what a house slave might do," said Mistress Phereby, and she reeled off a list of imaginary sins: "Your ma could throw away a piece of china to keep me from finding out that she broke it, or she could steal a silver spoon. Why, she could hide an egg in her sleeve and then cook it up for your dinner. If she does anything like that, you be sure to tell me, Ella."

She put a finger under the child's chin. "And here's the most important thing. Are you listening to me?" Ella nodded. She was having trouble following what her mistress was saying, but she understood perfectly well that she was just a slave, and she had to do as she was told.

"There's been talk. All kinds of talk. Why, just one county over, an ungrateful slave poisoned her mistress's food. If you hear your ma or any of the other slaves plotting against me, you be sure to tell me. Mind, now, this is to be our secret."

Ella knew she wasn't expected to reply.

"Because you are a good girl, you may look at this for a moment." Mistress Phereby handed Ella a kaleidoscope that was standing on an elegant table.

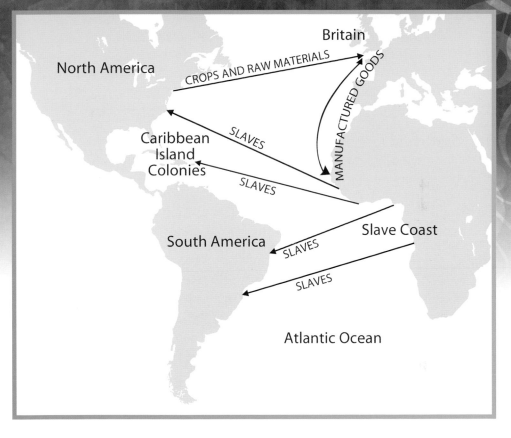

The Atlantic Slave Trade

Britain

North America

CROPS AND RAW MATERIALS

MANUFACTURED GOODS

Caribbean
Island
Colonies

SLAVES

SLAVES

Slave Coast

South America

SLAVES

SLAVES

Atlantic Ocean

Ella peered into the kaleidoscope, enchanted by the swirl-
ing patterns of brilliant blue and purple and red that formed
as she turned it. She wanted to turn it once more, but Mistress
Phereby snatched it out of her hands.

"That's enough for now," she said briskly. "When you have
something to tell me, you may look through it again. And
remember, what I've said is a secret!"

The Journey into Slavery

How did Africans become slaves? They were captured by rival tribes or African slave dealers, sold to European traders, and forced onto ships for a nightmarish voyage called the Middle Passage. "The place allotted for the sick Negroes is under the half deck, where they lie on the bare planks. By this means, those who are emaciated, frequently have their skin, and even their flesh, entirely rubbed off, by the motion of the ship…." wrote Alexander Falconbridge, a British surgeon who made four voyages on slave ships, in his book, *An Account of the Slave Trade in West Africa*. Many died during the voyage. Others were thrown alive into the sea because they were too weak to fetch a good price at auction.

The voyage from Africa to America was called the Middle Passage because it was the middle of a trade route that was more or less a triangle. On the first side of the triangle, boats carried textiles, guns, and brandy from Europe to Africa. These were exchanged for Africans captured and thrown into slavery, and this human cargo crossed the Atlantic to the Americas—the second side of the triangle—where the slaves were exchanged for sugar, tobacco, and cotton. The same ships then sailed the third leg of the triangle back to Europe. Almost everyone in the Western world had some connection to the slave trade, by producing raw materials, manufacturing the goods, or simply buying the products.

Captive Africans on the deck of the slave ship *Wildfire*.

Work in the cotton fields of the Deep South was back-breaking.

Nobody knows the actual numbers, but it is estimated that between the years 1500 and 1870 more than eleven million Africans were ripped from their homes, marched in shackles onto ships, and forced to live as slaves in a strange, hostile new world in South America, the Caribbean, and North America. Most of them lived in miserable conditions, forced to do back-breaking work and punished severely for the smallest offense.

After 1776, when the United States became an independent country, the "peculiar institution," as slavery was called, began to die out in the northern states. The businesses there did not require large numbers of laborers. But in the South, where cheap labor was needed to work the vast plantations of sugar, tobacco, rice, and cotton, slavery flourished.

The Hermitage, the plantation near Nashville where Ella Sheppard was born a slave. This print is from 1856, around the time that Ella's father was able to buy her.

Ella Sheppard and her mother, Sarah, were slaves at the Hermitage, a fine plantation that had been built by Andrew Jackson, who became the seventh president of the United States. It was a vast, prosperous place just outside Nashville, Tennessee, with a stately mansion, fields of cotton plants, and cabins where 150 slaves lived.

Ella's history was tangled up with that of the people who owned her. Her great-grandmother Rosa had been the daughter of a Cherokee chief. Rosa had fallen in love with the son of another chief—an African chief—who was a slave owned by Andrew Jackson's relatives, the Donelsons. Though Rosa had been born free, she loved her African chief so much that she was willing to live as a slave too. That is, except when the owners made Rosa angry. When she got mad enough, she'd stomp home to her tribe. Before leaving, she'd always threaten to lay a curse on the Donelsons if they harmed any of her fourteen children while she was gone. Sarah—Rosa's granddaughter and Ella's mother—was still owned by the Donelson family.

Ella's grandfather on her father's side was not a slave but a slave owner. He was a white planter named James Glover Sheppard. Slave women had no protection from their masters. If a slave-holder wanted to take one of his slaves to his bed, little could stop him. Many children on the plantations could say that their father was also their owner. One of James Sheppard's slaves had his baby, a bright, charming boy named Simon. James Sheppard also had a son, Benjamin, by his wife. Simon grew up as the slave of his own half-brother as well as his father.

When Benjamin Sheppard grew up and married Phereby Donelson, they both brought all their slaves, including Sarah and Simon, to the Hermitage. Simon became a livery man, working with the horses and carriages, and Sarah was a house slave.

Sarah and Simon fell in love. Benjamin Sheppard was fond of his half-brother, so he did something unusual for the time: he let Simon marry seventeen-year-old Sarah. Marriages among slaves weren't recognized as legal, and just about everybody, including his wife, Phereby, told Benjamin that he was being silly, but Benjamin thought that letting his slaves go through an imitation wedding ceremony was a harmless way to keep them happy.

On February 4, 1851, when Simon and Sarah's baby girl was born, the parents were allowed to name their own child. That was unusual too; slave owners had the right to name their slaves whatever they wanted. Sarah called the baby Samuella,

A nursemaid with her young charge, around 1850. The slave is dressed in formal clothing and the baby wears a christening gown.

Poole Art Co. NASHVILLE, TENN.

but it was a long name for such a scrawny little thing. From the first, she was called Ella.

Sarah Sheppard became Phereby Donelson Sheppard's most prized slave. She was in charge of the nursery and knew all the ways to make a house comfortable. She knew how to see to the oil lamps so that they never smoked up the room, and how to pour pitchers of water into Mistress Phereby's copper bathtub without soaking the polished wooden floor. She could mend a satin gown with tiny, even stitches, and she knew the secrets of lacing a corset tight enough to give her mistress a tiny wasp waist. She never spilled Mistress Phereby's night jar (toilet pot) when she emptied it. House slaves sometimes slept on thin pallets outside white people's bedroom doors, to be on hand day or night, but Sarah was so important that she had her own little room right next to Mistress Phereby's.

Though Phereby Sheppard valued Sarah, like most slave owners, she worried that her slaves would turn against her. That was why she asked Ella to report anything her own mother did. Strange as it was to ask a three-year-old to spy, it wasn't as odd as using a parrot for espionage; slave owners sometimes put parrots among their slaves, thinking that the birds would repeat suspicious words and let them know that trouble was brewing.

Almost everyone involved in the slave trade was obsessed with keeping control over the desperate, frightened slaves. They wanted control partly because slaves were expensive, and nobody wanted to lose one, any more than they wanted to lose a horse or a cow. But slave owners were also terrified that their slaves would rise up against them. They had good reason to be frightened. In Saint-Domingue (now Haiti), in 1791, slaves had carried out the bloodiest revolt in the New World, torching their masters' estates and hacking hundreds of white men, women, and children to death with machetes.

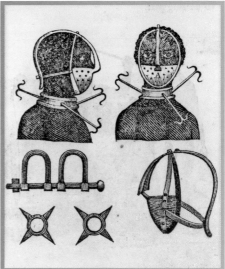

This woodcut shows the brutal iron mask, collar, leg shackles, and spurs a slave might be forced to wear.

A woodcut from 1831 shows horrific scenes from Nat Turner's rebellion. Slave-holders reacted by making conditions even harsher for their slaves.

The Life and Death of Nat Turner

Nat Turner, a slave in Virginia, was determined to revolt against slave-holders. On the night of August 21, 1831, he led a raid in which almost sixty white men, women, and children were massacred. Though Turner and sixteen people in his band were caught and hanged, his uprising terrified slave-holders all over the South. Their revenge was grim. Nat Turner could read, so there was a brutal crackdown on any slaves caught reading. Innocent blacks were killed for no reason, and their heads were displayed on roadsides as a warning to others who might have ideas of rebelling. Slave owners tightened every control they could think of, regardless of the suffering they caused.

Slave-holders thought that if they took away every shred of the lives their slaves had known in Africa, they would have more control over them. Families were broken apart: husbands and wives, children and parents, were sold away from one another. People from the same African tribes were split up so that they couldn't talk to each other in their own language, because talking might lead to plotting. They couldn't even keep their own names. Slave-holders sometimes picked names they found humorous; calling somebody who had no power Caesar or Prince was a sick joke. Other names were just plain mean: Teakettle, Mustard, or Donkey. A name like that was a message that the person who bore it wasn't quite human.

Despite all these efforts, slaves found clever ways to hold on to their old lives. When they could, they built their homes to look like the huts they had left behind in Africa. When there were no white people to hear, they called one another by their own names. When parents were sold away at slave auctions, the remaining slaves took care of the children, forming networks of people who considered themselves family.

The slave-holders also didn't allow their slaves to practice their traditional religions. They didn't approve of worship that used dancing and beating drums, and worried that drum-beats could send messages from plantation to plantation. The slaves got around this by holding secret "bush meetings" or "camp meetings." They would slip away after dark to "invisible churches" that might be no more than a marked tree in the forest. We still have descriptions of some of the songs they sang at such meetings, as early as 1700. These "corn ditties" were probably the earliest form of the songs we now call spirituals.

Slaves sang work songs to keep in time with one another on jobs like hoisting a heavy beam or rowing a barge, and to lighten the drudgery of picking cotton under a blazing sun or harvesting rice in a sweltering paddy. Religious songs were part of every prayer meeting, promising a home in heaven as the reward for a lifetime of suffering. And in the rare happy times, there were joyful songs for dancing. All this music—plantation songs, jubilees, and spirituals—was a rich part of the life that slaves struggled to forge for themselves.

Most whites either never heard this "slave music" or didn't pay attention to it, so the songs became a way to pass on secret messages. Somebody might let everyone know about a secret bush meeting by singing "Steal Away to Jesus." If a slave suspected that a white person had found out about the meeting, he could sing about "weevils in the wheat" to warn others to stay away.

The songs could also help slaves escape. Many tried to run away, though getting caught meant a vicious beating or even death. Those who did manage to get away traveled through swamps and rivers, where hounds couldn't track them, and headed north to freedom in a state where slavery was illegal, or on to Canada. Most of them couldn't have read a map even if they'd had one, so they relied on coded directions passed from one person to another in secret songs like "Wade in the Water" and "Follow the Drinking Gourd." ("Drinking gourd" was a code name for the Big Dipper, which would help fugitives find their way north by the stars.)

If they survived the snake-infested swamps and the bounty hunters, who hunted them for reward money, fugitives could find help on the Underground Railroad, a chain of courageous people, black and white, who risked their lives to offer runaways shelter, a warm meal, and directions to the next safe house. The Underground Railroad stretched right up to Canada, where slavery had been abolished years before. It might have been invisible, with no tracks and no trains, but the Railroad was as mighty as if it were made of steel.

For most slaves, however, the only escape was death, and Sarah very nearly chose that escape, for herself and her little girl. We don't know what story Ella had told Phereby Sheppard, but somehow Sarah found out that her daughter

Exhausted slaves escaping with the help of the Underground Railroad. Getting caught would have meant harsh punishment or even death.

had reported on her. She was horrified that her own child was being turned against her. Ella described what happened next: "In agony of soul and despair she caught me up in her arms, and while rushing to the river to end it all, was overtaken by Mammy Viney, who cried out, 'Don't do it, Honey! Don't you take that that you cannot give back.' She raised her eyes to Heaven and said, 'Look, Honey, don't you see the clouds of the Lord as they pass by? The Lord has got need of this child.'" The words of the old slave stopped Sarah in her tracks. She carried Ella up the path that led back to the house and to captivity.

For Ella, a future of hard work wasn't the worst part of slavery. She expected to grow up having to work, not because she was a slave but because she was poor. If you were a poor child, black or white, you almost certainly worked on a farm or in the mines or in a factory, or you were apprenticed to a tradesman. Half

This little girl is so small she has to stand on a box to reach her machine in a textile factory in Tennessee.

the workforce in the United States' textile mills was made up of children, some as young as seven. Ella's working life at the Hermitage might have started with cleaning away the bugs that gathered on windowsills, or fanning guests on very hot days. If she was lucky she would be spared one of the worst jobs for a child: standing behind the guests' chairs at formal meals. Having to stand perfectly still for hours was torture. But at least Phereby and Benjamin Sheppard weren't harsh or cruel slave owners; they weren't given to whipping or abusing their slaves. They never laid a hand on either Sarah or Ella.

For Ella, and for most slaves, the greatest fear was of being separated, usually forever, from the people they loved. Slaves

Slaves had many reasons to be afraid. The worst was the heartbreak of being "sold away."

THE PARTING "Buy us too."

could be sold to anyone, anywhere, without notice. Sarah said later, "From the cradle to the grave, the Negro woman lived in constant dread; no matter how favorably situated with kind and intelligent owners, there was no assurance that on tomorrow she would not be torn from her children and loved ones and sold to the coarsest and most illiterate master, and subjected to that from which only death could release her."

Most people who were born slaves died as slaves, but a small number did go free. Other than escaping, there were only three ways to become a "freedman." (The word referred to women and children as well as men.) Some slave-holders let their slaves keep chickens or grow vegetables or take outside jobs after they finished their regular work. They were allowed to keep any money they made, and by saving—sometimes for years—they might be able to buy themselves and be free. Others held jobs, usually in towns, but had to split their wages with their master. And a lucky few were simply freed, or "manumitted." A slave-holder on her deathbed might choose to free her slaves, in case having slaves turned out to be a strike against her getting into heaven.

Benjamin Sheppard decided to allow Simon to start his own livery stable in Nashville. Simon eventually owned several carriages and horses, and he bought his freedom from his white half-brother for $1,800.

In 1855, when Ella was still a small child, Phereby and Benjamin Sheppard announced that they were leaving the Hermitage. The whole household was moving to their plantation in Mississippi. But this time Sarah wasn't going with them. Simon had managed to raise another $1,300 to buy his wife and daughter. Sarah began to dream about what it would be like to be free, in a home of her own. That dream ended cruelly when she overheard Phereby admitting to her husband that, in truth, she had no intention of ever letting Simon buy Sarah's freedom. Her husband reminded Phereby that she had given her word to let Sarah go, but Phereby wouldn't budge. "She is mine and she will die mine!" she declared.

In a rage, Sarah confronted her mistress. Phereby's response? She said that she had known Sarah was bound to be upset when she found out she was going to Mississippi. Instead of making her miserable right away, Phereby claimed, she had generously given Sarah weeks of happiness by letting her think she'd be free!

We don't know if Phereby believed her own self-serving explanation, but Sarah certainly didn't. She knew what might lie ahead for her young daughter. Ella's earliest memory was of her "mother's tears over the cruelties of slavery, as she realized that its degradation fell heaviest upon the young Negro girl."

Sarah swore that if Phereby didn't at least let Simon take Ella, she would kill herself and her child. Phereby knew this wasn't an idle threat. In Nashville, when a woman had found out that she had been sold away from her children, she had called her three daughters to her, slit their throats, laid their bodies out side by side, and killed herself. Phereby gave in. She let Simon buy Ella for $350. Ella would lose her mother and live with her father in Nashville.

When the Sheppards arrived at the Mississippi plantation, the field slaves, half-starved and dressed in rags, were lined up along the drive to greet them. Phereby and Sarah were so appalled at their condition that they held each other and cried. For the next three years, mistress and slave would work side by side to improve food, shelter, and clothing for the slaves.

OH, FREEDOM

Oh, Freedom, Oh, Freedom, Oh, Freedom over me.
Before I'll be a slave, I'll be buried in my grave
And go home to my Lord and be Free.

Some historians claim that when Sarah Sheppard set out to drown herself and Ella, she sang the spiritual "Oh, Freedom" to her baby. Some even claim that she wrote the words. Wherever "Oh, Freedom" comes from, it follows the format of a spiritual, combining African rhythms with the structure of European music to create something brand-new. "Oh, Freedom" was a song of hope for those who wanted to escape slavery in this life and for those who dreamed of heaven. Like all spirituals, it has words that are easy to remember, it invites people to sing together, and it is packed with emotion. It is still sung to rally people to the cause of freedom.

Chapter 2

JOHN BROWN'S BODY

"When I done been to heaven, I's going to get my lesson, I's going to read, I's going to read my title clear."
— Levi Pollard, a former slave, quoting from an old hymn:
"When I can read my title clear/To mansions in the skies,/I bid farewell to every fear,/And wipe my weeping eyes." ("Reading one's title clear" means having the right to go to heaven.)

"I can tell you're scared, girl, and you're right to be so, on your first day at school. Only think about how lucky you are. I still have the scars on my legs from when I learned to read. I was about your age, I guess," said Cornelia. Cornelia was Ella's new stepmother. Shyly, Ella placed her small hand in Cornelia's as they walked to Mr. Wadkins's school. "Who taught you?" she asked Cornelia.

"Why, it was a tutor right from England. He came to the house to give the little master his lessons. In nice weather they would sit under the scuppernong arbor in the garden, and my job was to stand behind them fanning away the flies with a palm branch. They must have thought I had no eyes or ears, because it never occurred to anybody that I might be learning too. I knew better than to ask questions, but before I knew it, I could read and add up figures faster than the little master could.

"One day, the sun was blazing, so the little master's lesson ended early. He went up to the house, but he left his school-book behind. My brothers had been hoeing the garden nearby. I called them over, and we sat down in the shade to look at the book together. It was full of pictures of birds, I remember. They looked so alive they all but flew off those pages. I sounded out the names for my brothers.

Slaves like this unknown man (often incorrectly identified as John King) could suffer terrible punishments, like having their hands chopped off, if they were suspected of knowing how to read.

"The mistress must have seen us through the window. She came outside with a basket piled with sticks of peppermint candy and a big cold grin on her face. 'These are for you,' she said, 'if you'll only tell me which one of you is smart enough to read a book.' I was so green in those days, I stuck up my hand. Showing off, I guess. I thought she'd be proud of me. That earned me a whipping and a week locked up in the cold cellar." Seeing the fear in Ella's eyes, Cornelia laughed. "Oh, don't you worry. I'm not saying this to scare you, but to tell you I've never for one instant regretted knowing how to read. It's just the most wonderful thing you can learn!"

Ella was a reserved, gentle child, used to the quiet ways of the Hermitage, with its broad lawns and long alleys of cedar trees. Living in Nashville with her father, Ella found a very different world. The hubbub of Smoky Row, where Simon and most of Nashville's free blacks lived, bewildered her. Smoky Row was only a few square blocks, but there was so much to see. The higgledy-piggledy streets were lined with laundries, bathhouses, barbershops, blacksmiths, saloons, and livery stables. The air smelled of bread baking, fruits piled high on vendors' carts under the summer sun, and hot iron being forged into horseshoes. She learned to fall asleep to the boisterous sounds coming from the saloons, their doors propped open to let in fresh air.

Simon soon realized that he would never be allowed to buy Sarah, but he wanted a wife, and Ella needed a mother. Once again he scraped together some money, and he paid $1,300 for Cornelia Rohelia, a house slave. Ella never stopped missing her real mother, but she grew fond of kindly Cornelia.

Ella spent most of her time indoors because Smoky Row was a dangerous place. Despite the many lively businesses, the people were very poor and the place was crowded and filthy. Flies covered heaps of garbage and the bodies of dead dogs and cats. One by one, epidemics swept through: cholera, smallpox, and measles. Drunks and men on the prowl for prostitutes made the streets unsafe at night. The very name "Smoky Row" referred to people who were smoking opium and taking other drugs.

Kidnapping was the greatest danger of all. At the time Ella moved to Smoky Row, Nashville had ten slave auctioneers who bought slaves from Kentucky or sometimes from kidnappers who snatched blacks off the street. Being sold "down the river" meant being sent down the Mississippi to one of the large

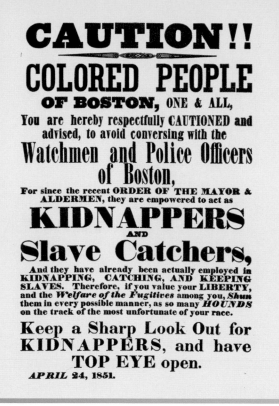

CAUTION!!

COLORED PEOPLE

OF BOSTON, ONE & ALL,

You are hereby respectfully CAUTIONED and advised, to avoid conversing with the

Watchmen and Police Officers of Boston,

For since the recent ORDER OF THE MAYOR & ALDERMEN, they are empowered to act as

KIDNAPPERS

AND

Slave Catchers,

And they have already been actually employed in KIDNAPPING, CATCHING, AND KEEPING SLAVES. Therefore, if you value your LIBERTY, and the *Welfare of the Fugitives* among you, *Shun* them in every possible manner, as so many *HOUNDS* on the track of the most unfortunate of your race.

Keep a Sharp Look Out for KIDNAPPERS, and have TOP EYE open.

APRIL 24, 1851.

This poster warns black people that the mayor has given the police and watchmen the power to act as slave catchers.

plantations in the Deep South, where there was an endless need for field hands to do the grueling work of picking cotton. Free blacks who were innocently going about their business could be carried off by force and sold into slavery.

Despite the poverty and danger, Nashville's black parents were determined to give their children a future. One way to do it was by starting schools. This was an extraordinary idea. After all, most poor children, regardless of color, seldom went to school. Their families needed the money they earned in the mills or needed their help in the fields. Abraham Lincoln, who would become president of the United States a few years later, had only thirty or so days of formal education, and that was in a "blab school"—a school where all the students chanted their lessons together.

Rich people had plenty of ways to give their children an education. They could send them to private schools in the United States or in England, or they could hire tutors to teach the children in their own homes. Nashville itself had many private schools, including a medical college and the fancy Academy for Young Ladies, but none of them would even consider taking a black student.

Learning to read was important: it meant someone could write a bill, send a letter to a loved one, or read a book or a newspaper. More than that, though, it was a mark of rebellion against the slave-holders, who used brutal methods to keep their slaves illiterate. Slaves who were discovered reading could be sold away, beaten or disfigured, or even executed.

There were exceptions: masters who allowed one or two of their slaves to learn enough reading to do their jobs. But even if slave-holders wanted their slaves to read, in most states they were forbidden by law. Reading was seen as the first step to violent revolution—after all, Nat Turner had been able to read. Slaves who could read could pass notes to one another and find ways to escape or, worse, to turn on their masters.

Freedmen in Tennessee were allowed to read but not to have schools. Time and again they asked for permission to open schools, but their request was always turned down. But they didn't give up; they opened schools anyway. Classes met in secret in church basements, in storerooms, even in people's attics.

As soon as they were settled in Nashville, Simon signed Ella up for Mr. Wadkins's school. Wadkins was a legend in Smoky Row. Thirty years before, a barber named Alonso

Proslavery rioters burn a Freedmen's Bureau school for black children in Memphis, Tennessee.

Summer had started a secret school for slaves as well as freedmen's children. When white people found out about the school, a gang descended on Summer and beat him so ferociously that he almost died. He ran off to Cincinnati and never came back.

Daniel Wadkins, the assistant barber in Summer's shop, vowed to carry on Summer's work. He hired a white teacher, thinking that would be safer for everybody, but he was wrong. The teacher was soon run out of town. Wadkins then took over the teaching himself. He would come to realize that both he and the teacher had been lucky. In Memphis, Tennessee, somebody had spread a rumor that white northern teachers were stirring up black students to revolt. In the melee that followed, a white policeman was killed. That was like a match thrown on dry straw. A white mob went on the rampage and for two nights Memphis was on fire. The mob burned down black churches, homes, and schools. All that was left was ashes.

Ella quickly learned the rules that kept anyone from discovering Mr. Wadkins's school. If a white person asked where she was going, she was not to answer. She was to take a different street every day so that nobody noticed her route. And she had to promise to keep track of the schedule. That was important because Wadkins was always changing the school hours, to confuse the authorities.

Wadkins was already an old man when Ella enrolled in his school. She described the lessons: "Each class stood up against the wall, head erect, hands down, toes straight. [We] spelled in unison, swaying from side to side, with perfect rhythmical precision, which we thought was grand…. [Mr. Wadkins's] eyes seemed to see everyone in the room, and woe to the one who giggled or was inattentive, whether pupil or visitor, for such a one constantly felt a whack from his long rattan [cane]." From the start, Ella loved school, and she grew to admire the cranky, brave Mr. Wadkins. But her happiness was short-lived.

In the neighboring state of Virginia, John Brown, a deeply religious white abolitionist, was preaching revolution. (Abolitionists wanted to abolish—end—slavery.) Brown believed that the Lord had called on him to free the slaves because owning slaves was a sin, and he did not want to live in a nation of sinners. He was different from most abolitionists because he believed in violence. He preached bloodshed as the only way to free the slaves, and he had already led a murderous raid that killed five supporters of slavery. Now Brown was resolved to create an army to take over the South by force. He and his men would begin by raiding a government weapons depot in Harpers

Ferry. But government troops overpowered Brown and his men. Several of his followers died in the gunfight, and the rest were hanged, along with Brown himself.

Reports from Harpers Ferry put everyone on edge. Whites were afraid of revolt, and blacks were afraid that whites would take revenge on them. Mr. Wadkins got death threats from people who claimed that his students were plotting a revolution

John Brown leaves jail on the morning he is executed.

like John Brown's. He was forced to close the school. Ella—who was about eight years old—was angry and disappointed.

In the weeks after the Harpers Ferry bloodbath, Nashville was tense and on edge. Ella couldn't escape tension at home, either. Simon's livery stable was failing. He sold one horse and carriage, and then another. He owed money everywhere. Ella and Cornelia weren't supposed to open the door anymore, in case it was one of Simon's creditors demanding to be paid. Then someone left a message that a creditor was coming to seize Cornelia.

Ella was horrified to learn that although Simon had bought her and Cornelia, he hadn't actually bought their freedom. He had never filled out the necessary legal documents, called manumission papers, that would declare both Cornelia and Ella to be free. As far as the law was concerned, his own child and his new wife were no more than his slaves, pieces of

Crowded Ragtown was host to many of the freedmen who lived in Cincinnati.

his property, like his horses and buggies. The people he owed money to had a claim on all his property, including Cornelia and Ella. They could both end up back in slavery. In a panic, Ella and Cornelia threw a few things into a battered trunk while Simon harnessed up the last of their horses. They headed north across the Ohio River to Cincinnati, in the state of Ohio, where slavery was illegal—where they could be free.

The Sheppards arrived in Cincinnati's Ragtown without a penny. Ragtown wasn't much different from Smoky Row, except that now Ella had to listen to the ceaseless sound of the ironworks, which set her teeth on edge. Simon hired himself out as a horse-cab driver and Cornelia took in washing. They squeezed boarders into their small house. They did whatever they could to make a little cash.

Though there were nights when their only dinner was biscuits sopped in salty gravy, somehow Simon managed to scrape together the money to buy Ella a piano. From the moment she touched the keys, she could play. The piano became her best friend. She spent hours playing, her slender fingers picking out melodies as she sang in her sweet, light soprano voice.

Stephen Foster and His Music

Some of the first songs Ella learned to play and sing were written by a young white man named Stephen Foster, who was to become the most popular songwriter in the United States. Though he is best remembered for his many ballads, he also composed "plantation songs" inspired by the songs he heard in Cincinnati when he strolled along the Ohio River, listening to the black dockworkers singing. His career was launched by "Oh! Susannah" (1848), a song that almost instantly became a hit with blacks and whites alike.

Simon also found the money to send Ella to school. She was bright and conscientious, a serious little girl who was eager to learn, but she was always sick. Ragtown was no cleaner than Smoky Row had been. The foul air was always damp, and the streets were full of garbage. Ella was plagued by coughs that she couldn't shake, and fevers that left her too weak to get out of bed. Eventually she couldn't go to school at all.

Cincinnati's citizens held a patchwork of opinions about slavery. In some ways, the city was at the heart of the northern anti-slavery movement. It was in the southern part of Ohio, right across the river from the slave state of Kentucky, so for years it had been a beacon for slaves escaping along the Underground Railroad. The city's abolitionists agreed that slavery was an evil that must be ended, but they disagreed about what should happen when it was over. Should ex-slaves stay in America, with all the rights of citizenship? Should they be helped to go back to Africa? What would happen to all these blacks if they were suddenly free?

While abolitionists argued among themselves, most people remained pro-slavery. Cincinnati had grown prosperous from trading goods with the South, and those goods depended on slave labor. Besides, almost every family had relatives in the South. How would their relatives survive if they lost all their slave workers? What could be done about these troublemakers who were upsetting things? Alonso Summer, the man who had started Mr. Wadkins's school, was one of the troublemakers. After he moved from Nashville to Cincinnati, he started a printing press. Perhaps he was printing abolitionist papers, or perhaps he was just guilty of being black. Whatever the reason, during one skirmish, a white mob burned down his business.

The Reverend Lyman Beecher. People often said that he and his large family of abolitionists were one of the best things about America.

The Extraordinary Beecher Family

People often said that if you had to pick the two best things about America, you'd have to say the flag and the Beechers. The family were strong abolitionists and were part of the Underground Railroad, sheltering many fugitive slaves on their way north. The school Ella attended in Cincinnati was an offshoot of Lane Academy, run by Lyman Beecher. Each of Lyman's seven sons became a preacher. One of them, Henry Ward Beecher, became the most famous preacher of his day. Catharine Beecher, one of Lyman's daughters, was a champion of women's education. Harriet Beecher Stowe, his other daughter, wrote *Uncle Tom's Cabin*, a heartrending novel that was a bombshell when it was published in 1852. It exposed the cruelty of slavery so dramatically that it changed public opinion. Many people believe that *Uncle Tom's Cabin* has had more social impact than any other American novel. The book has never been out of print.

JOHN BROWN'S BODY

John Brown's body lies a-mouldering in the grave
While weep the sons of bondage whom he ventured all to save;
But though he lost his life in struggling for the slave,
His truth is marching on.
Glory, glory hallelujah!
Glory, glory hallelujah!
Glory, glory hallelujah!
His truth is marching on!
He captured Harpers Ferry with his nineteen men so few,
And he frightened "Old Virginny" till she trembled through
and through.
They hung him for a traitor, themselves a traitor crew,
But his truth is marching on.

There are a great many versions and verses about the life and
death of John Brown. Whatever the exact details may have been,
there is no question that Brown's actions, and the stirring song
that commemorated them, became a rallying cry in the troubled
times ahead.

Chapter 3

WE ARE ALL IN THIS WAR

"We are all in this war, those who fight and those who stay at home."
—*a Pennsylvania newspaper, writing about the American Civil War*

On a frigid morning, Ella opened the front door and found a black woman and a small white child shivering on the stoop. She called for Cornelia and ran to pull the quilt from her bed. The woman and child curled up on the parlor floor by the fireplace and slept under the quilt all that day and all night. When they finally woke, Ella brought them tea. The woman warmed her hands on the cup and said, "My, oh my, this feels good."

Ella could hardly understand her thick drawl. "We've walked all the way from Alabama," the woman added, as the child gulped from the cup Ella held to her mouth. "When our master heard that Yankee soldiers were up the road, he got on his horse and rode away. The Yanks came and carried off what they could and burned the farm down around us."

"Her ma?" asked Cornelia quietly.

The woman stroked the child's hair, as fair as ducks' down. "Her ma suffered" was all she would say.

The South had grown rich thanks to slave labor, and southerners were determined that nothing was going to destroy their way of life. By 1861, slavery had been abolished in the northern states, where it had never been as widespread as in the South.

When southerners realized that slavery might be abolished in their states too, they began to secede (separate) from the United States.

The states that seceded joined together as the Confederate States of America (the Confederacy). The Confederacy declared that it was an independent country with its own president, Jefferson Davis, but the northern states were determined to keep all the states together as a single country. The two sides—the Confederacy and the Union—lined up against each other, ready to fight for what they believed in. The Confederate army came to be known as the Rebels, and Union soldiers were called Yankees.

The United States During the Civil War

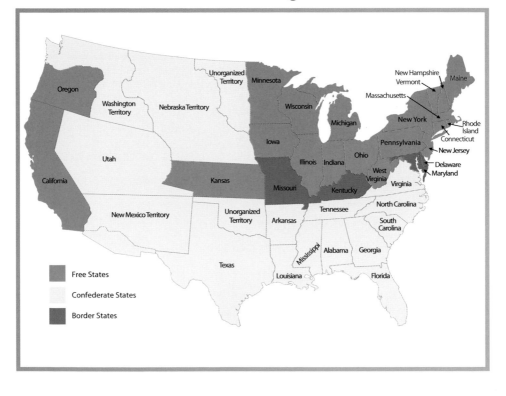

Confederate soldiers fire cannons, bombarding Fort Sumter in the distance. The attack on April 13, 1861, marked the start of the Civil War.

Fort Sumter, in Charleston, was South Carolina's harbor and proudly flew the Union flag. By March 1861, the fort was running out of food and other supplies. It would fall to the Confederate army if it didn't get help soon. Union supply ships set out from New York, but as they got near Charleston on the morning of April 12 they were bombarded by Rebel cannons. The Civil War had begun, and the armies were on the march.

The summer was almost over when news came that Cincinnati might be invaded by Confederate forces. Ella, who had just turned ten, saw the Cincinnati that she knew vanish almost overnight. Suddenly there were strangers everywhere. Some were refugees, black and white, who had fled north to stay a step ahead of the fighting. They were camped in every alley, with half-naked children squatting around little cooking fires. Others were soldiers. Thousands of men rushed into Cincinnati to defend the city. People called them Squirrel Hunters because instead of wearing army uniforms they dressed as if they were out for a day in the woods. They brought their own weapons with them: shotguns, hatchets, pistols, and squirrel rifles— whatever they had at home.

Simon Sheppard and the other freedmen in Ragtown were desperate to do their part for the Union. They sent a petition to the mayor, pleading for him to let them enlist in the Union army. At first the mayor turned them down, but it soon became clear that if Cincinnati was going to survive an attack, it would need all the help it could get.

Ella's father joined the Black Brigade, made up of hundreds of freedmen ready to lay down their lives to save their city from the Confederates. Ignoring the swarms of white boys who jeered at them, they marched to the hills surrounding the city, every day for months. With nothing but spades and broken shovels, the ragtag brigade dug eight miles of trenches where fighters could shelter while firing at Rebel forces. Protected by these defenses, Cincinnati was saved.

Every morning, in towns and cities both north and south, anxious parents, wives, and children gathered to read the lists of casualties nailed up at post offices, hoping that their loved one's name wasn't there. The bloodshed was staggering. In Tennessee alone, in 1862, the Union won the Battle of Fort Donelson, leaving almost 18,000 dead or wounded; the Battle of Shiloh, where 23,746 men died; and the Battle of Stones River, with 23,500 casualties. By the end of the war over 620,000 soldiers would be dead.

Terrified civilians—men, women, and children—were victims of the war.
This picture depicts Confederates destroying Lawrence, Kansas.

Civilians suffered too. Untold numbers died, mostly of disease or hunger. Food grew scarce and was often very expensive. People who lived near battlefields hid from the boom of guns and the screams of men and horses. Bloodied soldiers filled the hospitals, the cries of the dying carrying out to the surrounding streets. Everyone prayed for loved ones who were fighting, and for those caught in the path of the troops sweeping over the countryside. For blacks there was the added horror of a possible southern victory, which might enslave them again. When Ella ventured out of the house, she was always on the lookout for rogue Union soldiers, who were known to kidnap blacks and sell them to traders from the South.

Everyone everywhere wondered if the war would ever end.

"Honest Abe"

Abraham Lincoln was born into poverty in 1809. He worked as a shopkeeper and a postmaster, and even owned a general store, before he taught himself to be a lawyer. He was a great story-teller and had a warm way with people, which was helpful when he got involved in politics. His courage and integrity won him the nickname "Honest Abe." Lincoln disliked slavery, but he was willing to put up with it, at least temporarily, for the sake of keeping the country together. Although he was president for only a few years, he is remembered as the man who freed the slaves.

The text of the Emancipation Proclamation. Below the image of Abraham Lincoln are the figures of two women: one represents Justice and the other Liberty.

On September 22, 1862, President Abraham Lincoln met with his cabinet to read a document saying that if the Confederate states didn't come back to the Union, the goal of the Union would be to emancipate (free) all slaves. The black abolitionist Frederick Douglass said, "We shout for joy that we live to record this righteous decree." But the Confederates refused to rejoin the Union. They were willing to die rather than give up their slaves. After a sleepless night, his hand shaking as he held a gold pen, Lincoln finally signed the Emancipation Proclamation on January 1, 1863. It freed all slaves living in the rebel states. Lincoln declared, "In giving freedom to the slave, we assure freedom to the free—honorable alike in what we give, and what we preserve."

Frederick Douglass

Frederick Douglass was born into slavery; he grew up an orphan, never knowing who his father was. The dreadful abuse he suffered as a child slave made him a fierce abolitionist, and he fought slavery as a writer, speaker, activist, and also as part of the Underground Railroad. Having taught himself to read and write, he ran an anti-slavery newspaper and published a book about his experiences.

The signing of the Emancipation Proclamation took only a few strokes of Lincoln's pen, but slavery didn't end all at once. Some slave-holders tried to keep the news secret from their slaves, fearing that the slaves would take revenge on them if they found out they were free. Such efforts at secrecy were useless. News of the Emancipation Proclamation swept through the South. Some former slaves stayed where they were out of loyalty to kindly masters, or because they didn't want to leave

Refugees fled the South with nothing but a few belongings and the clothes they wore. Thousands died of cold and hunger.

loved ones, or because they were too weak or young or old to make the trek to safety. But thousands upon thousands fled.

Some slogged north through ice and mud with nothing but the tatters they wore because they were starving. Troops on both sides had destroyed plantations, churning up the neat fields, knocking down fences that had taken thousands of hours to build, and stripping the land bare of crops and livestock. Others left to get out of the line of fire when their plantations became battlefields. One former slave described how he'd been put to work burying dead soldiers from both sides or burning their bodies. When he found somebody not quite dead, he'd do him the favor of slitting his throat to save him from being burned alive. Yet others streamed north because they feared what would happen to them if the South won the war. Already they were feeling the revenge of outraged, panicking slaveholders. One refugee reported that his master had warned that

Dead Confederate soldiers lie in the ditch called "Bloody Lane," on the battlefield in Antietam, Maryland.

he would shoot every one of his slaves dead before he let them go free.

The first hastily clapped-together contraband camp was set up in Nashville to take care of women, children, and those men who were too weak to work. (At first "contraband" referred to runaway slaves, but it became the term for the roughly half-million blacks who flocked to Union lines for safety.) By the end of the war, contrabands lived wherever they thought they could find protection near Union outposts. The overcrowded camps were death traps. Thousands of contrabands froze, starved, or died of disease.

After the Emancipation Proclamation, blacks were finally allowed to enlist in the Union army. Immediately, several all-black regiments were formed. By the time the war was over, 180,000 blacks, both freedmen and former slaves, had fought against the Confederacy that was struggling so desperately to preserve slavery.

Gordon (we don't know his last name) is shown as a slave in ragged clothes, with scars on his back from beatings, and finally, wearing a uniform when he was allowed to become a Union soldier.

Officially, the war ended when the Confederate general Robert E. Lee surrendered to the Union general Ulysses S. Grant on April 10, 1865. But wars don't end just because people lay down their weapons. For weeks, battles flared up like the embers of a fire that wouldn't go out. And there were more deaths. Thousands of soldiers never reached their farms in the South or their hometowns in the North, dying from their wounds along the way. A riverboat caught fire, killing twelve hundred Union soldiers heading home. For years to come, farmers working their fields and children exploring the woods would find the skeletons of wounded soldiers who had crawled away to die alone. One victim was the most shocking of all. Just days after the South lost the war, Abraham Lincoln was shot to death by a southerner, John Wilkes Booth, while Lincoln watched a play with his wife. He was the first president in U.S. history to be assassinated.

Worn out from sorrow and fear and hardship, four million freed slaves had to find places to live and ways to feed themselves and their children. In March 1865, Congress created the Bureau of Refugees, Freedmen, and Abandoned Lands, known as the Freedmen's Bureau, to begin the huge task of feeding, housing, and clothing people left destitute by the war. Among other things, the Freedmen's Bureau was supposed to oversee three thousand schools for former slaves and to make sure that contracts between white landowners and black workers were respected.

Hungry people line up at the Freedmen's Bureau to receive food rations.

Refugees called "contrabands" fled north to escape the fighting. In this photo, taken in 1862, contrabands pose with Union soldiers.

The freedmen themselves began to rebuild their lives by rebuilding their families. In contraband camps, mass marriages created new families, while former slaves set about trying to reunite with their old families. Those who could afford the expense did everything they could to find loved ones who had been sold away from them. Heartbreaking ads appeared in newspapers like *The Colored Tennessean*, placed by former slaves looking for children or parents they hadn't seen in years.

The ads were mostly futile. For one thing, few blacks knew how to read. There was also the problem of names. Anybody who had been given an insulting name soon changed it. Others kept the surname of the last person to own them, not because they liked it but because it was convenient. Although the ads almost never brought results, the few reunions that did take place kept everybody hoping that a miracle might happen for them too.

As for Ella, once again, everything she knew was changing. She was fourteen when the war ended—no longer a child. What was she to do now?

BATTLE HYMN OF THE REPUBLIC

"John Brown's Body" was sung by Union soldiers, and another version was sung by Confederate soldiers. In 1861, a friend of the poet Julia Ward Howe told her that he thought more serious lyrics should be set to the same tune. Howe liked to say that she woke up one morning with all the words of a new version, the "Battle Hymn of the Republic," in her head. It became by far the most widely sung song of the Civil War. The lyrics have changed over the years, but this is the beginning of what she wrote in 1862:

Mine eyes have seen the glory of the coming of the Lord;
He is trampling out the vintage where the grapes of wrath are stored;
He hath loosed the fateful lightning of His terrible swift sword:
His truth is marching on.

I have seen Him in the watch-fires of a hundred circling camps,
They builded Him an altar in the evening dews and damps;
I can read His righteous sentence by the dim and flaring lamps;
His day is marching on.

The song ends by calling on people to follow the brave example of Jesus:

As he died to make men holy, let us die to make men free,
While God is marching on!

In a one-room school, a teacher is helping students identify different shapes. This hand-colored woodcut is from 1870, around the time Ella taught in Gallatin.

Chapter 4

GETTING INTO PARADISE

"I had the feeling that to get in a schoolhouse and study in this way would be about the same as getting into paradise."
—*Booker T. Washington, a famous black educator in his autobiography* Up from Slavery

lla picked her way around the puddles in the muddy schoolyard in Gallatin, fear cramping her heart. The school where she was to teach was nothing more than a windowless shack made out of logs, but it represented a huge amount of time and money to the impoverished freedmen who had built it. She pushed the door open. Three rows of crude wooden benches lined the walls. A stove and a battered desk stood at the front of the room. She picked up one of the few slates—the children would have to share. She looked around for books and paper. There were none.

Thirty-five children came to school the first day. One was not much more than a toddler; Ella had to pick him up and set him on the bench. Another brought along her own baby in a peach basket. Half the students were taller than Ella. One or two could read a few words, but most of them didn't know the alphabet.

By following Mr. Wadkins's lesson plan, Ella got through the first day. She had no discipline problems, as every one of the students was thirsty to learn. As she was tidying up the room after class, one of the biggest boys lingered in the doorway. "Thank the Lord that I have seen this day, ma'am. My master always said, 'Book learning don't grow no sugarcane.' He'd be mighty surprised to see me here."

Ella knew right then that that was all the thanks she'd ever need.

Simon Sheppard must have felt that he was doing well after the war because he sent Ella on a trip to Nashville. The Donelsons were visiting their old home, the Hermitage, and Ella had the chance to see Sarah, her real mother. There was a surprise waiting for her. Sarah now had another daughter, by a white man, so Ella had a three-year-old half-sister named Rosa. Sarah and her two daughters had three precious months to be close to each other.

That wasn't Ella's only trip, either. Simon treated her and Cornelia to a summer at beautiful Tawawa Springs, outside Cincinnati. There was a piano there for Ella to play and Bible study classes outside in the fresh, clean air. The very night

Ella Sheppard first met her half-sister, Rosa, right after the Civil War.

46

that Abraham Lincoln was assassinated, whites had set the camp building on fire, and Ella and Cornelia joined the volunteers who went to help rebuild it. While they were there, they received a terrible telegram. Disease was a fact of life in Ragtown. Ella had always been the frail one in the family, the one whose life they feared for. But it was Simon who had caught cholera. Now he was dead.

Neither Ella nor Cornelia had remotely suspected that Simon owed money again. They were shocked to learn that he owed more than they could possibly hope to repay. As soon as his creditors heard that Simon was dead, they descended on the stables and the house like locusts. They took away everything they could carry, even Ella's piano.

Once again, Cornelia and Ella were penniless. They packed up the few bits of clothing the creditors had let them keep and went back to Nashville. There, they took any job they could find. They scrubbed and ironed clothes, and lugged heavy baskets of clean laundry back to their customers. They found work as housemaids. They moved from a couple of rooms to one small, dingy one.

Music was Ella's only relief. She met a black photographer named James Presley Ball who recognized her talent and offered to pay for singing lessons for her. She agreed happily and began to study with Madame Caroline Revé, a white teacher who taught at the Glendale Female College. There was a catch: "I took twelve lessons in vocal music of Madame; was the only colored pupil; was not allowed to tell who my teacher was: and more than all that, I went in the back way, and received my lessons in a back room upstairs from nine to quarter of ten at night." But however furtive her lessons were, however hurt she may have felt, at least she was learning more about music.

For the first time, Ella's life was in her own hands. She was nobody's slave, and she wasn't under the kindly control of her father. But how should she get on with her life? She took stock. She was a hard worker, she had musical talent, and she believed Mammy Viney's prediction, so many years ago, that she had God's work to do. If she was going to put her gifts to use, Ella decided, she had to start with a good education.

Despite harsh conditions in contraband camps, schools were a priority for children who had had no chance to get an education when they were slaves.

Even before the Civil War was over, the members of the American Missionary Association, the AMA, were starting schools all over the South, believing that blacks could only be truly free if they had an education. Before Emancipation, the schools had to be secret. Even after they were permitted, few people were willing to rent or sell space that would be used to educate blacks. The AMA had to take any premises it could find. That's how the Fisk Free Colored School, in Nashville,

Clinton Bowen Fisk crusaded for
education rights for black people.

came to be housed in twenty yellowing buildings that had been thrown together during the war to serve as a military hospital.

The school was named in honor of a decorated Union general, Clinton Bowen Fisk. General Fisk worked for the new Freedmen's Bureau. He himself had grown up hungry and too poor to go to school. With good luck and a lot of work, he had become a wealthy banker who counted Abraham Lincoln and the leader of the Union army, General Ulysses S. Grant, among his friends. Maybe because he'd had no chance of getting an education himself, he became a crusader for the right of black people to go to school.

The AMISTAD and the AMA

Twelve years before Ella was born, forty-nine men and four children were sold to slave traders in Africa and taken to Cuba. They managed to take control of the ship, the *Amistad*, and ordered the crew to sail back to Africa. Instead, the crew sailed to New York City, where the Africans were put on trial. The case went right up to the U.S. Supreme Court, where at last they were declared free to go back to Africa. The group that came together to defend the people of the *Amistad* helped form the American Missionary Association. Fired by the belief that it was a sin for humans to enslave one another, they set up missions for run-away slaves in Canada, for freed slaves in Jamaica and Hawaii, and for Chinese immigrants in California. Even before the Civil War, the AMA believed that the way to freedom was through education, and in the face of violent and often deadly opposition they opened schools throughout the South.

Ella set her sights on Fisk, but first she had to earn the eight dollars she needed for tuition. She answered an ad to teach in a school for black children in Gallatin, Tennessee. Gallatin was a small, hardscrabble town that had been overrun by contrabands and soldiers during the war. By the time they moved on, there wasn't an apple left to pick or a chicken left to cook.

It took enormous courage for a black girl of fifteen to become a teacher, because schools had become the new race battleground. All over the South, poor whites who had lived their whole lives peaceably among black people found them-selves competing with former slaves for scarce jobs. Rich whites wanted their old way of life back, supported by slaves in the house and in the fields. Many southerners, rich and poor alike, felt humiliated that they had been defeated and bitter about their losses. From that stew of suspicion, anger, and frustration, southern newspapers conjured up a new evil: the Black Threat.

The Ku Klux Klan set out on a campaign of terror. In this drawing from 1872, a Klansman is aiming a rifle at a defenseless family.

They spread fear of the revenge that could fall on whites if black people became their equals. And the blacks' surest route to equality was education.

Groups with names like the Order of the Pale Face and the Order of Zoroaster formed, determined to bring back the old ways. But the most notorious group sprang up first in Pulaski, Tennessee. It called itself the Ku Klux Klan, from the Greek word for "circle," and its goal was to make sure that no black person could ever carry a weapon or cast a vote. Members hid their identities under hoods to spread their terror. Their weapons were secrecy, the noose, and fire. They threatened; they burned crosses; they beat their victims or lynched them from a handy tree.

An editorial cartoon by Thomas Nast illustrates how racist groups made the black experience after the Civil War as fraught as ever.

Davie Jeems and the Ku Klux Klan

While many of the Klan's tactics were savage, some were just weird. Wanting to spread fear by pretending to be the ghosts of dead Confederate soldiers, Klansmen sent former slave Davie Jeems this threatening note, spelled and punctuated as it appears here, in 1868:

> NOTICE
>
> To Jeems, Davie. you.must.be.a good boy. and. Quit. Hunting on Sunday and shooting your gun in the night. you keep people from sleeping. I live in a big rock above the Ford of the Creek. I went from Lincoln County during the War I was Killed at Manassus in 1861. I am here now as a Locust in the day Time and at night I am a Ku Klux sent here to look after you and all the rest of the radicals and make you know your place. I have got my eye on you every day, I am at the Ford of the creek every evening from Sundown till dark I want to meet you there next Saturday … We have a Box for … you. We nail all, radicals up in Boxes and send them away to KKK-there is 200,000 ded men retured to this country.

The Klan saved a special kind of fury for black political leaders, teachers, preachers, and anybody white who helped set up a school. In North Carolina, the Klan was so violent that forty-nine schools had to close. In 1866, all twelve of the black schoolhouses in Mississippi were burned down. No student or teacher was safe. Teachers were whipped or even branded.

The hate groups did all this because, like the former slaves, they knew that education meant power. They were determined to keep that power out of black hands. Ella was well aware of this danger, but she was willing to face it so that she could get an education for herself. She also believed that it was what God wanted for her. Her faith inspired and comforted her.

Ella didn't stay in Gallatin long. She would have lasted, despite the long hours and even the constant fear, if only she'd been able to make money. But though the tuition was only a few pennies, often the students couldn't pay it. She found that by the end of five months she'd only been able to put away six dollars. It was hard to say goodbye to her students, but she had to find another way to make a future for herself. She went back to Nashville and did sewing and other jobs, but by the time she had paid for rent and food there was nothing left. At this rate, she would never get to Fisk. What could she do?

Ella might not have had tuition money, but she had no shortage of determination. She arrived at Fisk in September 1868, boldly asked for the person in charge, and asked if she could enroll in exchange for work. The man in charge, big, blustery George Leonard White, told her that her savings would buy her only three weeks. Besides, there was already a long waiting list of others willing to work instead of paying tuition. But Ella was so resolutely persistent that he finally relented.

Ella moved in to the dormitory with so little luggage that the other students teased that her tin trunk was nothing but a pie box. She didn't tell anybody that her trunk was not only small but half-empty.

Fisk demanded a lot from its teachers and its students. The teachers were white, and mostly northerners who had come to Fisk to do what they believed to be God's work. That belief kept them strong even when the whites of Nashville shunned them or refused to rent them lodgings. The school had to provide rooms for them but couldn't afford much else. Teachers had to bring all their own things, including mosquito nets and as much food as they could carry. They preserved fruits and vegetables to stretch out the meager dinners. They even split kindling, hauled coal, and built the fires in all the common rooms, the only rooms that had any heat. Students wore their coats in icy classrooms to save on fuel.

Students and teachers alike tried to cope with the buildings, which were falling down around them. The military hospital was not built to be permanent. Ella described the dormitories: "So many of us shivered through … winter with not an inch of flannel upon our bodies … the wind whistled around and groaned so fearfully that we trembled in horror in our beds, thinking the sounds were the cries of lost spirits of the soldiers who had died in them."

The teachers at Fisk were the first white people Ella had ever really known, other than Madame Revé and the Sheppards at the Hermitage. It took her some time to relax in the company of these well-meaning northerners. Then there was the matter of accents. The teachers had a hard time understanding her southern drawl, and she couldn't understand their rapid Yankee twang.

The only easy part of life was the schoolwork, not because it wasn't challenging—it was—but because everyone was so glad to be getting the education their parents had been denied. The strict schedule appealed to Ella's sense of order. She studied from five-thirty to seven in the morning, went to classes during the day, and studied again from six-thirty to nine at night. Between classes she taught three private music students, helped

Fisk had a strict set of rules and regulations for the way students were expected to behave.

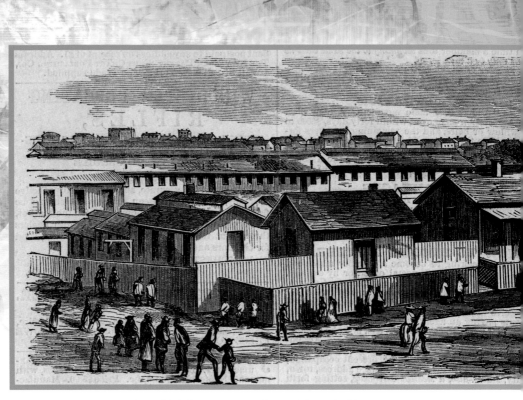

An early engraving of the Fisk Free Colored School founded in 1866.

to serve meals, washed dishes, wiped tables, and took in sewing to pay her way. When her cough made her too sick to sit by the window to sew, she propped her back against her pillows and sewed in bed.

One day, when some students were working out on the grounds, they found links of chain poking through the hard-packed dirt. They realized with a chill where they were. Right up to the Civil War, this had been Porter's Slave Yard—a place of heartbreaking sorrow where men, women, and children were auctioned off as if they were livestock. The chains that lay rusting under the dirt were the shackles that had cut into the wrists and ankles of the captives. Tears blurred the students' eyes, but they forced themselves to keep digging. They sold the chains for scrap metal and used the money to buy schoolbooks and Bibles.

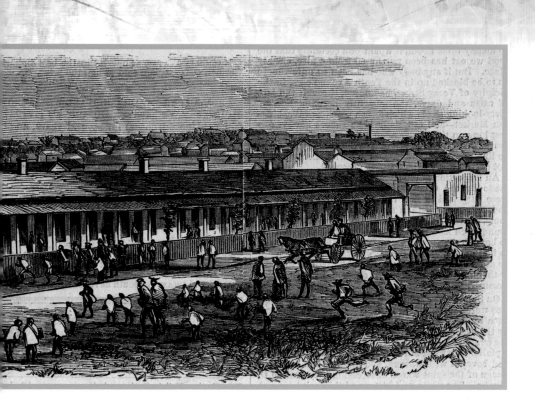

Despite the long hours, the endless scrimping, and her poor health, Ella had never been happier. To her delight, she found that music was part of everyday life at Fisk, thanks to George Leonard White. He was from a poor white family in Michigan and had left school at fourteen to teach. He had gotten into trouble right away by organizing a Sunday school for black children. Wearing his black schoolmaster suit, with a Bible tucked in his pocket, he had been one of the Squirrel Hunters who defended Cincinnati.

Despite being disorganized and terrible with details, White took on the wretched job of treasurer at Fisk. His real passion was music. Though he had never had a music lesson, he taught himself to play the fiddle. His own singing voice was a low croak, but there was nothing he loved better than the sound of voices blending together, and he was a good choirmaster.

From George White's first day at Fisk, he encouraged students to sing together at lunchtime or in his apartment in the evening. He even wrote away to the AMA for musical scores, arguing that the students would be learning hymns while they learned to read music. He knew the best music happened late at night, when the students gathered to sing spirituals, the plantation songs they'd learned when they were slaves. Often, George White would lean against the doorway to listen to them, tears in his eyes.

Not long after Ella came to Fisk, White heard her playing the piano and singing in the women's hall. Tiny, quiet, self-controlled Ella and fly-off-the-handle White, tall as a tree, became odd musical partners, but they were best friends from the start. Within months, White had made Ella the music teacher at Fisk. She was only eighteen when she became the first black faculty member in the school's history.

George White was always trying to find money for Fisk. It occurred to him that a performance by students might be a good fund-raiser, and Ella agreed. Before they did anything else, however, they had to get permission from the new head of the school, Adam Spence. Spence was a serious, God-fearing man, so much so that nobody had ever seen him laugh. He didn't have any ideas of his own to raise money, but at first he didn't like White's plan because it would take students away from their schoolwork. After a lot of arguing, he gave in: "It will encourage the colored people and it will lift them into respect with others," he said.

But what music should they perform? Mr. White and Ella picked a modern cantata, a story told in song, named *Esther, the Beautiful Queen*. Ella started to learn all the parts so that she

In the image, handwritten names appear: Minnie Tate, Green Evans, Isaac Dickerson, Jennie Jackson, Maggie Porter, Ella Sheppard, Benj. M. Holmes, Thos. Rutling, Eliza Walker

A postcard showing the original Jubilee Singers. Seated, left to right: Minnie Tate, Greene Evans, Jennie Jackson, Ella Sheppard, Benjamin Holmes, and Eliza Walker. Standing, left to right: Isaac Dickerson, Maggie Porter, and Thomas Rutling.

could help assemble a choir and direct it. The choir had to be made up of sopranos for the higher women's parts, contraltos for the lower women's parts, tenors for the higher male parts, and basses for the lower male parts.

Next, she and White invited singers to join the choir. They asked Maggie Porter, one of Fisk's first students, if she would sing the soprano role of Queen Esther. Maggie had grown up as a slave in Nashville. When she was very little, she said, "I began sitting on the curb to listen to the choir with my feet in the gutter. Finally, I got courage enough to sit on the last step and listen to the music, and the leader asked me if I wanted to hear the music." Some people told White that a girl with skin as dark as Maggie's couldn't possibly be the heroine, but

Maggie shrugged off the comments. She'd heard much worse. By the time she got to Fisk, she'd been a teacher in three small schools. When she'd come back to the last school from Christmas vacation, there had been nothing left but its charred skeleton. The Ku Klux Klan had celebrated Christmas by burning down a school.

Isaac Dickerson was chosen for his booming bass voice. Isaac's first memory was of watching a slave trader buy his father. His mother had died young, so from the age of five he'd had to raise himself. After Emancipation he'd gone to Chattanooga, taking any kind of work he could find. A Jewish shopkeeper had seen promise in the boy and had taught him to read. That taste of learning was all it took. Isaac went on to a missionary school and eventually he started to teach. His school was one of the ones torched in the Memphis riots.

The other bass was Greene Evans. He had been born on a plantation owned by the richest man in the county. When the slave-holder found out that Yankee soldiers were getting close, he rounded up fifty of his slaves, including fourteen-year-old Greene, and ran away. For two years the whole group moved from place to place, always one step ahead of Union troops. Greene and his brother got separated from the others somewhere in Alabama. They were whacking their way through the underbrush when they heard the sounds of soldiers. They emerged right into a Yankee army encampment. The commander took a liking to Greene, gave him a job, and encouraged him when Greene announced that he had saved enough money to enroll in Fisk.

Craggy-faced, intense Benjamin Holmes was a deacon of Fisk's chapel. He had a sharp, quick mind and a tenor voice as smooth as honey. As a small child he had been apprenticed to

Greene Evans, one of the original members of the choir.

GREENE EVANS.

Photographed by BLACK.   Page 69.

a tailor in Charleston, South Carolina. Every time he was sent on an errand, he studied the signs painted on shop windows. When he felt brave enough, he'd ask a kind-looking person to read him the words. By the time he was twelve, he could read the signs himself. When it looked as if Charleston was going to be captured by Union troops, Benjamin's master was furious. He had paid good money for his slaves and he'd lose it all if they were set free, so he sold them to a slave trader. The slave trader stored his "inventory" in prison until he could find buyers. Benjamin was sitting in prison when he got hold of a newspaper and read about the Emancipation Proclamation. It didn't do him any good at first—he was still locked up behind bars—but he was freed when Charleston finally fell. Like Ella, he'd taught in a small country school. One day when his students were reciting their lessons, someone had shot a rifle through the window. The bullet whizzed by Benjamin, just missing his head.

The other tenor was "Rollicking" Thomas (Tom) Rutling. George White and Ella had debated whether Tom should be asked to join the choir. He'd nearly been expelled from Fisk because of his fondness for passing notes to girls. But he had the best tenor voice they'd ever heard, so, along with stern warnings, he got a place in the cast. Tom's first memory was of his mother being dragged away, wailing, while her scared children watched helplessly from the doorstep. He heard she'd tried to escape and had nearly died from a whipping when she was caught. That was the last news he ever had of his mother. When Tom was eight, he was put to work behind a plow. The rest of the time he was a house slave, fetching wood and carrying pails of water almost as heavy as he was. During the war, the master had warned him not to repeat any news that he heard when he was waiting on the family. Tom had promised solemnly, but as soon as he could get away he had told the other slaves everything he knew.

Tom had learned about the Emancipation Proclamation while he was serving dinner. The next morning, the master rode out to the slave quarters and announced that everybody was free to go. At first they all whooped with joy. Then it hit them: they had nowhere to go. They stayed on the plantation for two more years, doing the same work as before, only now the master claimed that he was paying them wages by giving them food and a place to live. Tom and his brother finally left because an older sister in Nashville sent for them. He was shining shoes there when he met an army surgeon who encouraged him to go to the Fisk Free Colored School.

Jennie Jackson was beautiful, with very dark skin, and she had a soprano so pure that it made Ella's heart ache. She would be wonderful on the stage. Like Ella's, Jennie's story began at the Hermitage. Jennie's grandfather had been the personal servant of President Andrew Jackson, so she shared the president's

"Rollicking" Tom Rutling was especially popular with the ladies.

THOMAS RUTLING.

surname. Jennie's mother had been set free when her owner was on her deathbed, but the man taking care of the will had tried to burn the papers. In a panic, Jennie's mother had fled to Nashville with her daughter.

Seventeen-year-old contralto Phebe Anderson's father was a minister. He doted on his daughter and was willing to let her go to Fisk, but he demanded that the teachers promise to tell him if she got any love letters.

Fifteen-year-old Georgia Gordon's grandmother, Nancy Duke, was a member of a prominent North Carolina family that had made a fortune growing tobacco. When Nancy's kin found out that she had eloped with her own slave, a fiddler named Bill, they disowned her. As a child, Georgia had been shielded from racism by her family, but when she got older she began to realize what it meant to be of mixed race. She felt that she didn't fit in with either white society or black society.

Finally, there was Minnie. Small, sweet-faced Minnie Tate had a contralto voice so rich that it was hard to believe she was only thirteen. Minnie hadn't had the same hard times as the others. Her grandmother and her mother had been set free by their master in Mississippi. That was no guarantee that they'd stay free—they might be captured and sold again—so they set off on foot for Ohio, where they'd heard they'd be safe. They had no idea how far away Ohio was, or even where it was. Many times they had to stop along the way to find work in order to buy food. Eventually they came to a town in Tennessee where the people, most of them German immigrants, welcomed them so warmly that they decided to settle there. Minnie had grown up never knowing what it was like to be a slave.

Dressed in lavish costumes, the cast performed *Esther, the Beautiful Queen* in Nashville and again in Memphis, for audiences of enthusiastic missionaries and church members. Mr. White was jubilant. *Esther* made money for the school. And Ella, who had taught the singers their parts, rehearsed them, and played the organ during the performances, got her first reviews.

"Miss Shepard [*sic*] … played with true artistic touch, showing consummate skill and taste, as well as a thorough knowledge of musical rules," reported one newspaper. Another wrote that she made "as favorable an impression for her modest yet self-possessed manners as almost any one [*sic*] that we remember."

Esther, the Beautiful Queen brought in welcome dollars, but not enough to make a lasting difference. Just when Adam Spence and George White didn't think their financial woes could get worse, they did. Teachers weren't being paid so they threatened to leave. Local merchants refused to sell them food until they paid their past bills. Mr. White was so tormented by stress that he was doubled over from stomach cramps. Fisk owed two thousand dollars, a huge sum in 1870. The Fisk Free Colored School was about to close.

SWING LOW, SWEET CHARIOT

Swing low, sweet chariot,
Coming for to carry me home;
Swing low, sweet chariot,
Coming for to carry me home.

I looked over Jordan
And what did I see,
Coming for to carry me home?
I saw a band of angels coming after me,
Coming for to carry me home.

"Swing Low, Sweet Chariot" was Ella Sheppard's favorite spiritual. We don't know who wrote it (some claim that it was written by Sarah Sheppard), but its message that slaves would find a home in heaven, no matter how hard their earthly life might be, was a comfort. It may also carry a secret message. It was one of Harriet Tubman's favorite songs. Tubman was a slave who managed to escape in 1849, and then returned to the South eighteen times to lead around three hundred slaves to freedom. She was so successful that eventually a reward of $40,000 was offered for her capture. Legend has it that if somebody sang "Swing Low," it meant that Harriet Tubman would be arriving soon to lead a slave to freedom.

Harriet Tubman led hundreds of slaves to freedom on the Underground Railroad. She is more than ninety years old in this photo.

65

Chapter 5

ROOT, HOG, OR DIE

*"It's time to root, hog, or die. I'm depending
on God, not you."*
— George White

*("Root, hog, or die" was a popular phrase from the
1830s. When a hog was released in the woods, it
was told to root for food for itself if it wanted to
live. The phrase means "be self-reliant.")*

The students performed *Esther, the Beautiful Queen*
again in Memphis, but this time the audience was
disappointingly small. The singers stood glumly outside a small hotel at the station, waiting for the train that would
take them home to Nashville. Ella was so tired that at first she
didn't notice the angry white men gathering around them. The
men swore at Mr. White and called the girls vile names, and the
singers looked at each other in dismay. Blacks could be beaten
or lynched for the smallest reason, or for no reason at all. They
had no weapons, no way of protecting themselves. Or so they
thought.

Coolly, Mr. White turned to the students. "Would you be
kind enough to favor these gentlemen with a song?" Ella never
forgot what happened next. She wrote, "Our hearts were fear-
ful and tender and darkness was falling. We were softly finish-
ing the last verse of 'Beyond the Smiling and Weeping' when
we saw the bull's eye of the coming engine and knew that we
were saved. The leader begged us with tears falling to sing the
hymn again, which we did."

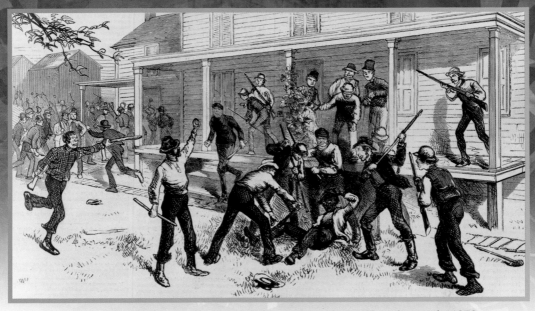
White men beat a black man to death in Patenburg, New Jersey, in 1872.

George White was worried sick. The school was out of money and there were no more corners to cut. The roofs were leaking. The rations were so scanty that students and teachers were dropping out from malnutrition. White was paying the grocer out of his own pocket. In desperation, the students put on *Esther, the Beautiful Queen* yet again. The takings were slim, only a few hundred dollars, but the concert gave White a daring idea. If they could make a little money on one performance, maybe they could make a lot of money if they gave a lot of concerts. They would go on tour.

He outlined his plans to Ella. They already had a choir—the cast of *Esther*. And they already had a route—they would follow the stops on the old Underground Railroad, starting in Cincinnati, Ohio, because they'd be able to count on abolitionist ministers to lend them their churches. The concerts in the churches would be free, but after each one they would pass

Minstrel Shows and "Blackface"

In 1843, in New York City, a white performer named Thomas "Daddy" Rice smeared burnt cork on his face and put on rags to do a song-and-dance routine mocking Jim Crow, a character in many slave stories. Rice was such a hit that other white singers, dancers, and comedians put on similar "blackface" to give minstrel shows. White audiences loved them. A minstrel troupe even sang at the White House.

What the audiences didn't realize was that they were watching a joke inside a joke. For instance, some minstrel player always strutted around doing a step called the cakewalk. White audiences thought this was a fine mockery of the way black people walked. In fact, the cakewalk was an imitation of how blacks thought *white* people walked. So whites were laughing at other whites pretending to be blacks, who were imitating blacks imitating whites!

Unfortunately, the minstrel shows weren't just harmless amusement. They took smoldering prejudices and fanned them into flame, encouraging audiences to tell themselves that black people really were like the shifty, lazy, stupid, happy-go-lucky minstrel characters they laughed at on stage. Audiences could go home with renewed confidence that such buffoons didn't deserve or even want equal treatment.

Thomas "Daddy" Rice in
his minstrel costume.

the hat to gather up donations. From Ohio they would go to Pennsylvania, New Jersey, and then New York.

White and Ella wanted a program that would show off the students as talented, dignified young ladies and gentlemen, so they chose serious music: pieces from *Esther*, some hymns, a sad ballad or two by Stephen Foster, and even a song that George White himself had written. This concert would give audiences a whole new idea of who black people were and what they could do, very different from the demeaning minstrel shows that were the rage. Mr. White would organize the travel. As well as singing, Ella would be in charge of rehearsing the choir and leading them during performances.

Performers do the cakewalk in Primrose & West's Big Minstrels, a troupe of white people pretending to be black.

Even though she didn't have much confidence in Mr. White's organizing abilities, Ella loved the idea of touring from the start; she saw it as God's mission for reaching people's hearts.

But for what sounded like such a good idea, it stirred up a hornet's nest of bad feeling at Fisk.

First, there were objections from the AMA. Its members didn't want to provide the up-front funds to pay for travel and hotels, funds that White promised would be paid back from the profits. They worried that there would be no profits, leaving the school worse off than before. White turned to General Fisk himself. Not only did the general say no, but he advised them to give up the plan in case it brought disgrace on everybody at Fisk. After all, performing was not considered to be respectable work. And who knew what a group of teenagers would get up to?

Then there were the other teachers. They had poured so much effort into their students, and here was a plan that would cost them months of school.

The final straw was a skirmish between one of the best singers, Georgia Gordon, and George White. In a huff, she quit the choir. That infuriated White. He responded by kicking her out of Fisk altogether.

But the strongest opposition came from the parents of the singers. Only Minnie and Georgia had never been slaves. To the parents of the others, the thought of traveling brought back terrible memories. Slaves had traveled when they were sold away. Travel meant separation and suffering. Understandably, they were afraid for their children. From the time Fisk opened, students had been targets for local whites who resented seeing them marching to school. Almost every day, somebody was hit by a stone or punched. How safe would their children be, standing helpless in front of an audience of white strangers?

All summer long Mr. White and Ella argued with the parents. The parents only gave in when White promised that he

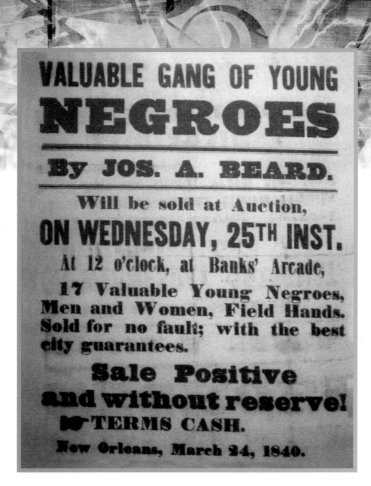

VALUABLE GANG OF YOUNG
NEGROES
By JOS. A. BEARD.
Will be sold at Auction,
ON WEDNESDAY, 25TH INST.
At 12 o'clock, at Banks' Arcade,
17 Valuable Young Negroes, Men and Women, Field Hands. Sold for no fault; with the best city guarantees.
Sale Positive and without reserve!
☞TERMS CASH.
New Orleans, March 24, 1840.

An auction notice advertises the sale of a group of young people. Such a sale usually meant a lifelong separation from loved ones.

would hire a chaperone. That seemed reasonable to everyone, but it proved to be a headache. Not one Fisk teacher was willing to take the job for what they thought was a doomed mission.

At last, the unflappable Mary Wells sent a message that she'd come along as a chaperone. Mary was a serene missionary with the nerves of a gladiator. When she had announced that she was dedicating her life to helping black people, her wealthy family in Michigan had promptly disowned her. After serving as a Union nurse in the Civil War, she had moved to Athens, Alabama, to teach in a black school. One night when she was marking papers, Klansmen surrounded the small building and shot a bullet that whizzed right by her and lodged in the door. Mary refused to let the Klan intimidate her. She didn't hide. She didn't even put out her lamp. She just went on marking papers. The students kept that door as a reminder of her bravery—until the Klan came back and burned the school down.

So now they had a chaperone, but there was one small catch. Mary would only come if she could bring her black ward, Georgie. Georgie was just eight, but he'd known a lifetime's worth of hardship. His mother had died when he was a baby. Two runaway slaves had taken him with them as they fled from their burning plantation, but as soon as they got to a Union camp, they deposited him with the soldiers and took off. Barely old enough to walk, Georgie had entertained the soldiers by tumbling and singing for them. They had kept him alive by feeding him bits of army rations and coffee.

The troops left Georgie behind when they moved on, and nobody bothered to question the farmer who offered to take him in. The farmer tied the little boy to the gate leading into his fields to scare away crows and left him there. Georgie wasn't about to be a human scarecrow so he gnawed through the rope and ran away, but he had nowhere to go. By the time some kind soul found him, lying near the railroad tracks, he was close to death. But Georgie had heard the name Mary Wells somewhere, and he whispered to his rescuer that he wanted to be taken to her. Mary could no more turn her back on a starving child than she could fly. Since then, Georgie had been her son. Now, he became part of the tour.

The night before the singers left, Adam Spence invited them to his rooms to pray. Ella looked from one expectant face to another. Four of the singers had been among the first students at Fisk: Maggie Porter, Jennie Jackson, Eliza Walker, and Thomas Rutling. Each of them had come through some form of hell to get to Fisk, and Ella felt as protective of them as a mother lion. These were the people who would save Fisk—or lose it. She bowed her head as Adam Spence prayed, "Oh Lord, if this thought comes from Thee, prosper the going out of these young people. Care for and protect them, and bring them back to us bearing their sheaves with them, and we shall give Thee the glory."

The Choir, October 1871 to March 1872

Phebe Anderson, contralto
Isaac Dickerson, bass
Greene Evans, bass
Benjamin Holmes, tenor
Jennie Jackson, soprano
Maggie Porter, soprano
Thomas Rutling, tenor
Minnie Tate, contralto
Eliza Walker, contralto
Georgie Wells, performer
Ella Sheppard, soprano and choir mistress

Ella wrote about the morning they left Nashville: "Not one of us had an overcoat or wrap. Mr. White had an old gray shawl … Taking every cent he had, all his school treasury could spare, and all he could borrow, and leaving his invalid wife and two small children … Mr. White … started. In God's strength, October 6, 1871, with his little band of singers to sing the money out of the heart and pockets of the people."

Mr. White had bought first-class train tickets for the choir. This wasn't a luxury. The other cars were notorious: full of

Train travel was crowded, noisy, and uncomfortable for most passengers. It was much worse in the "smoking cars," where passengers were often drunk and rowdy.

drunks, black and white, who were likely to harass girls, especially black teenagers, and blue with cigar smoke that could damage their voices. Just as the students were looking for their seats, however, a train official stopped them and ordered them to ride in the smoking car with the drunks. They might be dedicated students, they might be talented musicians, but they were black. To some people, that was still the only thing that mattered.

The train ride was dismal for both Ella and Mr. White. They stared out the window, thinking of their first trip to Cincinnati—White with his musket and Bible, and Ella escaping from debtors who wanted to sell her into slavery.

GET ON BOARD

CHORUS
Get on board, little children,
Get on board.
Get on board, little children,
There's room for many a-more.

VERSES
The gospel train's a-coming,
I hear it just at hand;
I hear the wheels a-rumbling,
And rolling through the land.

The fare is cheap and all can go.
The rich and poor are there.
No second class aboard this train,
No difference in the fare.

Over and over, the singers would be treated badly on trains, so when they published this song in 1872, in one of their first songbooks, it had special meaning for them. Though the song sounds like a spiritual, the original version probably came from the pen of a northern Baptist minister at the beginning of the Civil War. It is still sung as an anthem about equality.

Chapter 6

SONGS FOR THE RIGHT

We have songs for the gay and cheerful,
We have songs for the rich and the poor;
We have songs for the sad and the tearful,
And songs for the RIGHT ever more.
— an advertising flyer for the choir, written by George White

W hen the choir reached Cincinnati, George White left everyone in the train station while he went in search of lodgings. He was soon back, announcing that they had rooms in a boarding house just down the road. They carried their few belongings to the lodgings, unpacked, and washed their faces. White handed around slabs of bread and cheese, and new fall apples, and they set out to explore.

They noticed signs leading to a nearby exhibition. The centerpiece of the exhibition's music display was a shiny grand piano that anybody could try out. Mr. White nudged Ella, but her fingers were already itching to play. She smoothed her skirt, rubbed her hands to warm them, and ran her fingers lightly over the keys. She struck a chord and sang the first verse of a song she loved, "Annie Laurie." One by one, people stopped to stare. Soon a crowd had gathered around the piano, astonished to see a black woman playing a wistful Scottish folk song so beautifully. Ella, who had a knack for pacing, wanted a show-stopper as the next song. The choir joined her for "The Star-Spangled Banner," and the crowd was won over. This accidental concert was the best possible publicity, especially because the choir had almost no money for advertising. In no time, they had an invitation to sing to a church congregation the next day.

George White,
friend and
champion of the
Jubilee Singers.

The singers had all been on stage before, but they were still
nervous before the first concert of the tour. They waited silently
in a small cloakroom off the church's social hall, listening to the
sound of shoes clattering on the wooden floor as the audience
filed in. Ella heard an odd noise. Were Isaac's teeth chattering?
No, his knees were knocking. But it was too late to reassure
him. It was time to take their places. She gave the singers the
key for the first hymn, "Children, You'll Be Called On," and
she tipped her head slightly. That was their cue to begin. She
glanced at Isaac. Once he started singing, he relaxed. They hit
every note in perfect harmony.

The concert was over quickly. Before they knew it, the audience was clapping. The singers stood at attention as Mr. White
walked onto the stage. "Thank you for your generous applause
for these fine young people," he said. "I hope you will be as generous with your coins. They are on a mission to secure the future

of their school." Georgie walked between the rows, carrying a bowl, but while the audience had been generous with their applause, they were not so generous with their pocketbooks. The choir made almost nothing from that first concert.

Ella was proud of how well they had sung, but she suspected that the audience saw them as freaks. She could hear their remarks as they filed out of the hall. One woman laughed at their prim, modest clothes and claimed they were playing dress-up in "white people attire." A man admitted that they sang European music well but said he'd been hoping for a minstrel show.

No wonder he was disappointed. Except for Georgie's dancing and telling a few stories for comic relief, there had been nothing in their program that anyone could confuse with a minstrel show. Ella and Mr. White were determined that the singers would appear not as buffoons but as they really were: dignified, intelligent, and gifted.

Their next stop, in Chillicothe, Ohio, gave them their first bitter taste of northern prejudice. The singers dragged themselves after Mr. White from hotel to hotel, trying to find anyone willing to rent rooms to them. Finally, the only place left to try was the shabby American Hotel. The landlord offered them his own back bedroom, with the warning that they weren't to go into the dining room in case any of his other guests saw them. When Georgie passed the bowl that night he only collected thirty dollars, barely enough to pay for their train tickets and lodgings.

The next day, the whole country was caught up in news from Chicago. The city, built mostly of wood, was on fire, and three hundred people had died in the flames. Almost a hundred thousand saw their homes and everything they owned burn

After the singers gave their first concert, they learned that fire had swept through Chicago, leaving thousands homeless. They donated their concert earnings to the victims of the fire.

to the ground. The singers voted to send every penny they'd earned in Chillicothe to Chicago, to help the victims of the fire.

The singers fell into a rhythm as they traveled through Ohio. Every morning they had a prayer meeting. George White sometimes went ahead to the next town to meet with ministers, to scout out places to give concerts, and to do what little advertising he could afford. Every now and then a newspaper wrote a good review, and that helped bring in audiences.

Ella rehearsed the choir every day. Because they had no place else to practice, they had to rehearse in their hotel rooms. She knew that nobody needed much of an excuse to throw them out, so she taught them one of the most difficult skills in choral singing—how to sing softly but powerfully at the same time. It is especially hard for a choir to hit the first note of a song softly. Mr. White had once told them to think about a tiger: "You might not hear its tread behind you, but the power is there all the same."

Finding places to spend the night was a constant worry. They'd been prepared to stay in fleabag hotels or boarding houses because most entertainers—song-and-dance acts, magicians, actors—stayed in them. Such places were called don't-look-under-the-bed rooms, meaning that you wouldn't want to think about the rats or the roaches you'd find there. Many times, the singers couldn't even get into such flophouses. They would wait in the train station while one of the boys or Mr. White trudged through the cold from hotel to hotel, looking for any place that would take black guests. When they didn't succeed, they would go from door to door in black neighborhoods, asking strangers if they could make room for one or two of the singers overnight.

On the nights when nothing worked, the singers would sit on the hard benches in the train station, huddled in shawls, as they counted the minutes until morning. Ella wrote, "Many times would we have given up in despair had it not been for our noble friend Mr. White. He in the midst of suffering cheered us on our mission, saying 'he had too much faith in God to fail in so great a work.'"

The singers were growing more discouraged every day. Ella wrote, "Many a time, our audiences in large halls were discouragingly slim, our strength was failing under the ill treatment at hotels, and on railroads, from poorly attended concerts, and ridicule; besides, we were too thinly clad for the increasing cold

NEW PASSENGER STATION, CINCINNATI, O.

In the nineteenth century, seven railroad companies operated in Cincinnati out of five stations scattered across the city. Most connecting passengers (and their baggage) had to change stations. There were many plans for a new station, but those plans were delayed because the seven companies couldn't agree on where it should be or who should pay for it.

of a northern climate." Their neat clothes were becoming worn and dirty. Mr. White had to borrow money from Minnie Tate and from his family to buy the men winter coats. Mary Wells, the chaperone, gave Ella a warm cloak.

They tried to drum up interest by singing on street corners. They adjusted the program to bring in audiences that had little patience for the kind of serious music George White liked. Audiences roared for more when little Georgie sang and danced, or did impersonations of country preachers. That helped bring in more people but not more donations.

Word got back to Nashville that the tour was turning out to be a disaster. The choir lost Phebe. Her father, the doting minister, was very sick, and he sent for her. In Cleveland, they couldn't even find a place to perform. Adam Spence's panicky letters to White didn't help. Spence blamed White's foolish tour idea for the end of the Fisk school itself.

The original meeting house in the First Church in Oberlin looks much the same as it did when the Jubilee Singers performed there. First Church is a City of Oberlin Historic Landmark, and it is on the National Register of Historic Places.

George White booked the singers to perform at the First Church in Oberlin, Ohio, where the National Congregational Council, a collection of important church leaders and ministers, was meeting. Even before they got there, the singers were on edge. Oberlin was a town of just three thousand people, and five hundred delegates were coming to the meeting. What chance did the singers have of finding a hotel? To their relief, Oberlin's black community put them up in their homes. They hoped this was a good sign.

By the time they plodded through gray sleet to the First Church, the hems of the girls' long wool skirts were caked in slush. The business part of the conference was still taking place as they found seats in the gallery, as quietly as they could. They peeled off their wet woolen mittens and wiggled their icy toes in their soggy boots.

One endless speech followed another. Ella fished around in her bag for a bottle of cough syrup and took a swig before she passed it to the others. They had almost dozed off, from boredom and the heat of the packed room, by the time the business meeting droned to its end. Now the ministers were stretching and chatting to one another in the aisles. They ignored the chairman as he called out, "Patience, please! One more moment! Just one more moment of your time! Would you mind listening to these youngsters from Fisk? They were all slaves and now they're here to raise money."

Mr. White and Ella had decided that this time they wouldn't start with a European hymn or a piece of classical music. Instead, the choir began with the first hushed note of "Steal Away." None of the ministers paid any attention. The choir watched Ella and she raised her fingers. That was the signal to start building the sound to a crescendo. One by one, the ministers fell silent and sat back down. Soon the church was throbbing with the power of the choir's voices. Then, as softly as they'd begun, they sang the last note. It floated on the air, clear and pure.

For a moment the audience sat in silence, while Ella and Mr. White exchanged worried looks. Then the applause began.

From the moment she first touched a piano, Ella could play.
She spent hours accompanying herself as she sang Stephen
Foster songs and the Scottish ballads she loved.

It rolled over them in waves. The ministers stomped their feet
and cheered. They mopped their teary faces with their handker-
chiefs. Ella sent up a silent prayer of thanks, and she too had
tears running down her cheeks.

Many good things came from the concert in Oberlin. The singers made $130 in donations, and one of the Beechers, Thomas,
promised that he would write to his famous brother, Henry
Ward Beecher, in New York. If the singers could just make it to
that city, Henry would see to it that they were a success. Most
importantly, the singers had seen what happened when they sang
"Steal Away." It was one of their old secret songs and the only
plantation song they sang that day. Ella wrote, "The slave songs
were associated with slavery and the dark past, and represented

the things to be forgotten. They were sacred to our parents. We did not dream of ever using them in public. It was only after months that gradually our hearts were opened to the wonderful beauty and power of our songs." After seeing the amazing effect it had on the audience, they decided that, from then on, they would include as many spirituals as they could in the program.

This was not as easy as it sounds. It meant building up a list of songs, and then dividing the melody into voices for different parts of the choir to sing. They started by sharing the songs they already knew. Ella described the work: "To recall and to learn of each other the slave songs demanded much labor, and to prepare them for public singing required much rehearsing."

How Choral Singing Comes Together

Choral, or choir, singing is not the same as having a sing-along with friends. Human voices can range from very high to very low, and choirs are made up of singers to cover each range. Choral music is divided into four parts: soprano, alto (or contralto), tenor, and bass. A good choir asks its singers to sing in the range that's comfortable for them. There's no point expecting a soprano to aim for the deep bell sounds of the bass or asking an alto to reach the high notes of a soprano.

Choir members have to have really good hearing and great timing. It's very difficult to stick to your own part when people around you are singing different notes. Each person has to know precisely when to start and finish—no stragglers allowed. And the voices have to blend. Nobody's voice should stick out, except in a solo.

Ella had to know every part, and she had to be able to teach singers to sing as well as possible. On stage, she led the choir so subtly that the audience didn't notice. She would just tip her head or raise a finger slightly as a signal when the tempo slowed down or sped up, the sound level changed, or a different voice was to join in.

Every song had a memory attached to it. Ella had learned "Swing Low, Sweet Chariot" from her mother, Sarah. Jennie's mother had sung "Gabriel's Trumpet's Going to Blow" while she scrubbed white people's clothes on her washboard. Tom had sung "I Ain't Got Weary Yet" to himself when he was a young boy trudging along the furrows behind a plow bigger than he was.

When they ran out of songs they already knew, they asked anybody else who might possibly know a plantation song to share it with them. When they learned of an old lady in St. Louis who knew some of the earliest songs, Jennie Jackson took a train to Missouri to meet her and memorized thirty songs she'd never heard before. Ella wrote down the words and musical notations so that not a note would be lost.

Now that so many of the spirituals have lost their original meaning and appeal to us simply as beautiful songs to sing with our friends, it is hard to imagine how much courage it took to perform them for the first time to white audiences. In the days of hotels that barred blacks, of schools surrounded by armed guards, and of the ever-present danger of being lynched, to sing "Steal Away" or "Oh, Freedom" was an act of sheer bravery.

Yet every time they performed the spirituals, audiences who had never been farther south than Cleveland sang along with the choruses or stamped their feet in time. They couldn't get enough of this amazing music.

The choir left Oberlin with fresh energy, but it faded once they were back on the road. They faced the same dreary problems: hotel rooms that smelled of cat pee and cabbage, or no rooms at all; rude taunts at train stations; nearly empty concert halls. They were troubled by coughs, sore throats, and aching joints

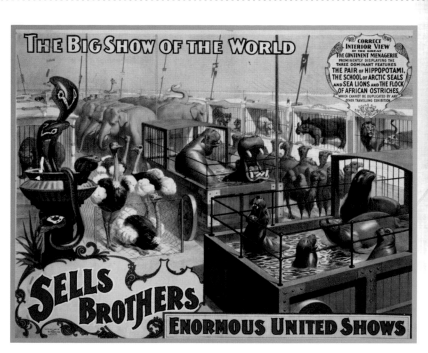

The Jubilee Singers were competing with other kinds of popular entertainment, like the Sells Brothers' The Big Show of the World.

Show Business, 1870s style

When the Jubilee Singers toured, they were competing for audiences against many other kinds of entertainment. Minstrel shows were the most popular, but people could also go to the circus; to a freak show to gawk at those with physical disabilities; to Wild West shows to marvel at trick riding and shooting; or to tent shows. Tent shows were especially popular in the countryside. They consisted of a short play with songs and dancing between acts. Being an entertainer didn't have the status it does today, and it certainly didn't make you a celebrity. Some people thought entertaining was not quite proper work for ladies and gentlemen.

from the damp late autumn weather. After somebody mistook eighteen-year-old Ella for fourteen- year-old Minnie's mother, Ella peered into a pocket mirror. The dark smudges under her eyes did indeed make her look like an old woman. She wasn't one to share her feelings, but she was so low that she wrote to Adam Spence back at Fisk: "Did you ever think I had a secret sorrow hidden beneath my seemingly happy countenance? Well, such is the case. How often I have wanted to lay my weary heart to rest in the quiet grave—but I must work and try to make others happy. I am young and weary of life." Then, afraid she'd said too much, she pleaded with Spence to keep her complaints private.

The choir didn't know what to do. Should they quit and return to Nashville, or should they risk going on to New York? If they failed there, they wouldn't even have enough money to get back home. One night in Columbus, Ohio, they prayed together to find an answer. It came the next morning. "Mr. White met with us with a glowing face," wrote Ella. "He had remained in prayer all night alone with God. 'Children,' he said, 'it shall be Jubilee Singers in memory of the Jewish year of Jubilee.'"

Jubilee was an ancient Jewish practice. Every fifty years all debts were forgiven, all fields left unplowed, and all slaves set free. Jubilee meant freedom and celebration all at once. (The word "jubilee" comes from a Hebrew term for a ram's-horn trumpet.) Ella knew right away that it was the perfect name for their group. "The dignity of the name appealed to us. At our usual family worship that morning there was great rejoicing." Now that they had just the right name, they were resolved not to give up.

The Hebrew term for a ram's-horn
trumpet, called a shofar, is the source
of the word "jubilee."

Their rejoicing lasted only until the next town, where
they had to borrow money to pay for their decrepit rooms
"over a porch that was so rickety we had to lean to the wall to
keep from falling. We found the room so well-occupied [with
insects] that a part of us only could sleep while the others slew
the occupants."

By the time they got to Pennsylvania, Ella's southern blood
was rebelling against the icy wind and the dirty snow and the
gray sky. Her cold feet were a constant torment. She'd worn
through her shoes. All she had left to wear were thin woolen
slippers that soaked up the rain and sleet. She couldn't speak
without hacking into her handkerchief. A doctor told her that
if she wanted to get well, she had to go home. Ella didn't bother
with an answer. The choir had become her home. They would
push on to New York together.

STEAL AWAY

CHORUS LINE
Steal away, steal away, steal away to Jesus!
Steal away, steal away home.
I ain't got long to stay here.

VERSE
My Lord calls me,
He calls me by the thunder;
The trumpet sounds within my soul:
I ain't got long to stay here.

"Steal Away" can have many meanings. It can refer to being resigned to the burden of slavery in this world while the singer longs for heaven. Sometimes, though, it was a signal that an escape to freedom was being planned.

Chapter 7

SING UP THE WALLS

"The work done by this group of singers is without a parallel. It leaves the Old Testament hopelessly in the distance, for Joshua's army only sang down the walls of Jericho, while the Jubilee choir have sung up the walls of a great university."
— *Henry Ward Beecher*

"This must be the place." Mary looked at the slip of paper in her mittened hand. "The Continental Hotel. Wait with the luggage. I'll be quick." The Jubilees stamped their cold feet in a dark street in Newark, New Jersey, while Mary Wells registered them and got the room keys.

For once, the rooms were clean. A fire crackled in the fireplace. "Those sheets sure look inviting. Do we have time for a nap? I want to warm up." Maggie stretched out on one of the beds. Ella was rubbing her freezing feet when the girls heard somebody pounding on the door of the room next to theirs.

Cautiously, they looked out. Ben stood in the hallway with a very angry white man. "I am the manager. I have been duped! I was told you were singers. Minstrels! You aren't minstrels at all!" The man swabbed his shining forehead with his handkerchief. "You're colored folk!"

Ben replied mildly, "We may not be minstrels, but we're sure singers. And yes, we're colored."

George White came puffing up the stairs, dragging his trunk behind him. "Is there a problem?"

The manager made it clear that he was not about to have real black entertainers in his establishment, only entertainers in blackface.

Mr. White tried to reason with him. "My good man, it's late. I assure you, you won't find quieter or cleaner guests. We will leave in the morning."

The manager looked them over with hard, unsmiling eyes. "OUT!"

It was too late to try to find another hotel, so they trudged back to the train station in the dark. Suddenly a stranger reined in his horse beside them. "What now?" said Tom.

"Are you the Jubilee Singers?" the rider asked. "I've heard about what just happened. Don't think we're all as plug-ignorant as that fool!"

Somehow, all of Newark had learned that the Jubilee Singers had been thrown out of the Continental Hotel. Apologetic townspeople rallied to offer the singers their own rooms. That night, the choir slept in some of the grandest homes in town.

When the Jubilee Singers arrived in New York, they found a city still impoverished from the Civil War. There wasn't even enough money to repair broken sewers.

The first thing the Jubes, as the Jubilees called themselves, noticed when they got off the train in New York City was the smell. The war had left the city too poor to pick up the mountains of festering garbage or to fix the broken sewer pipes. The foul smell matched their mood. They were tired, cold, and tense. Everything depended on how they did here in New York. If they failed, the school would be bankrupt, and they would be blamed for wasting its last precious dollars.

Ella and Mr. White went over their program again and again. Little Georgie had had such a bad throat infection that Mary Wells had taken him home to Alabama, so there wasn't a whiff of a minstrel show left in their performance. They would be singing their favorite spirituals.

Henry Ward Beecher, a preacher who changed the fate of the Jubilee Singers.

The man who would determine their fate was Henry Ward Beecher. His jutting chin and squat body made him look like a grumpy bulldog, but people adored him. He was the most famous preacher in the United States, in the days when preachers were major public figures. The people who attended his church, the Plymouth Church in Brooklyn, were the cream of high society. After getting his brother Thomas's letter about the Jubilees, Beecher had invited the Jubilee Singers to perform at the prayer service he held every Friday in the church's lecture hall. He wouldn't tell anybody ahead of time; the singers would be a surprise for his congregation.

This was a risk, and the Jubes knew it. New York was in the North, but it had a long, twisted history with slavery. "Blackbirders" (slave smugglers) had used the port to sneak in slaves long after slave trading was against the law in the North. Many of the New Yorkers at the Plymouth Church had made their fortunes by shipping southern goods like cotton, rice, and

The slave market on New York City's waterfront was gone by the time the Jubilees visited, but "blackbirders" (slave smugglers) continued to operate long after slavery was illegal there.

New York also had a strong abolitionist tradition. This illustration shows people in Syracuse, New York, rescuing a runaway slave from those trying to catch him.

tobacco to Europe and the rest of the world. The abolition of slavery had been a severe blow to their prosperous businesses, and they might not warm to a choir of former slaves.

Beecher had the Jubes hide behind a curtain in the church's loft. They peered out through a slit at the hall below, crowded with mustached gentlemen and silk-clad ladies carrying flowers. Beecher himself sat at the front in a big velvet armchair, receiving the bouquets his congregants offered him.

A clock chimed and the genteel babble died down. Beecher took one last sniff of a rose, stood up, and introduced the singers in a commanding voice: "Hear the songs that have been sung by generations of benighted souls, on the plantation, by day and by night—songs that have enabled the captive to endure his chains, the mother to hope against hope and to keep her soul up …" With that, the curtains parted. The startled audience looked up at the gallery.

The Plymouth Church in Brooklyn.

Backs straight and heads held high, the Jubilees sang the first soft note of "Steal Away." The rows of elegant ladies and gentlemen sat spellbound as the choir sang one spiritual after another. Before the last note faded away, Beecher was on his feet, bouncing on his short legs. "They may be nightingales, but even nightingales have to eat!" he shouted. With a flourish, he reached into his pocket and waved a five-dollar bill. "Let me be the first to make a donation!" That day, the Jubilee Singers raised $250.

The afternoon at Plymouth Church made the singers a sensation. They gave concerts all over New York. They were invited to sing in New England. In Hartford, the governor of Connecticut attended, as did Samuel Clemens, better known as Mark Twain. Twain became one of the choir's biggest fans, and he described the Jubilees' singing in a letter: "I think these

The most powerful members of high society were
members of Henry Ward Beecher's church.

gentlemen and ladies make eloquent music—and what is much
to the point, they reproduce the true melody of the plantations,
and are the only persons I ever heard accomplish this on a
public platform …. It was the first time in twenty-five or thirty
years, that I had heard such songs, or heard them sung in the
genuine old way—and it is a way, I think, that white people
cannot imitate—and never can for that matter, for one must
have been a slave himself in order to feel what that life was and
so convey the pathos of it in the music."

An illustration from *Adventures of Huckleberry Finn* by Mark Twain. Mark Twain, one of the United States' most important writers, was a great supporter of the Jubilee Singers.

Mark Twain

Samuel Langhorne Clemens spent his childhood in Hannibal, Missouri, on the banks of the Mississippi. He left school when he was twelve, soon after his father died, and at fifteen he went to work as a printer on his brother's newspaper. He later became a ship's pilot on the Mississippi. During the Civil War, river trade all but stopped, so he went back to working with newspapers, this time as a journalist. He took his pen name, Mark Twain, from a pilot's term meaning that the river is deep enough (at two fathoms—"twain" means "two") to navigate. Twain went on to write many newspaper articles and short stories, and twenty-eight novels, including *The Adventures of Tom Sawyer* and *Adventures of Huckleberry Finn*. He is still considered one of America's finest writers.

Once again, Ella's life turned upside down. She had been a slave, then a survivor of the Civil War, living in the eye of that bloody storm, then an impoverished laundress. She had taught in a school targeted by the Ku Klux Klan, she had become Fisk's first black teacher, and now she was the leader of a choir of stars. She wrote to Adam Spence, back at Fisk, "Our only fear is that this grand success will turn our heads, but I hope with the help of your prayer that we may feel all the more humble to our Leader above for this glorious success. We are petted and loved and flattered by everyone we meet. Yet I personally am the humble Ella that I was when I left."

When Ella wrote that the Jubilee Singers were loved by everyone, she wasn't including newspaper reviewers. The highbrow critics, judging the choir by the conventional standards of the day, were cruel. The *New York World* called the singers "trained monkeys." Papers ran reviews claiming that only those who didn't know anything about *real* music could possibly be impressed by the Jubilees.

Though critics wrote them off as a novelty act, serious musicians were excited about what they heard. "The slaves of the South came to begin a totally new history …," declared one source. "We have never heard voices which were blended in a harmony so absolute. With no accessory of dress, with no stage manners, or claptrap of any kind, they have simply thrilled audiences…. The most remarkable part of their singing is in the 'Praise songs' they bring out of their old slave life."

Despite all the sold-out concerts and all the praise, the Jubes learned quickly that success was not a shield against popular prejudice. They still drew rude comments on the street about black people getting "uppity." They were still turned away from hotels, in case white guests complained about having to rest their heads on pillows that blacks had used. The difference was that now there was sometimes an outcry, a protest against this mindless racism, as there had been in Newark. Still, they were surprised when they found prejudice in the most unexpected places.

When the singers were back in New York to give a concert at Steinway Hall, General Fisk himself came to New York to introduce them one by one. The general started with Tom Rutling, and the audience chuckled when he said, "Tom's cash evaluation was once $450. Now I think you would agree with me that he is worth at least $500!" Next, he drew Minnie Tate forward from the row of girls. "This is Minnie. She could have been bought for $350. Once you hear that voice of hers, you'll agree that at $1,000 she'd be a bargain."

The Jubilees had already seen a newspaper review that described Tom as "Negro man, very black, six feet high, worth in old times $2,000 under the hammer—basso." Now they were hearing the same ugly joke from someone who was supposed to be their champion. The general surely didn't mean to be cruel. He thought he was making a little joke to amuse the audience. But his remarks were a horrible reminder of the long, dark years when black people were just possessions, to be bought and sold at will. Despite the uncomfortable introduction, the singers—as always—gave the best performance they could.

By May 1872, the Jubilee Singers had raised twenty thousand dollars for Fisk. It was enough for the school to stay open. As a bonus, they had collected all kinds of useful donations from northern business owners: clocks for the classrooms, silverware for the dining hall, Parker Brothers pens for each student, gas fixtures, even a bell carved with the singers' names.

The singers logged hundreds of miles on trains.

All that was left for them to do was get on the train and go home to Nashville in triumph. Once again, Mr. White bought first-class tickets for them all. But when they had to change trains in Louisville, Kentucky, the door of the first-class waiting room flew open and a red-faced railway worker planted himself in front of them. Spit flying, he ordered them out onto the platform. White got to his feet and pulled himself up straight so that he stood looking down at the little man. "These, sir, are our tickets!" He waved them in the man's face.

A policeman appeared and grabbed Jennie by the arm. "What's the trouble here?" The people in the first-class waiting room stared at them. Outside, on the platform, a surly group was gathering. Mr. White gave in. But this time, once the train arrived, an embarrassed conductor led them to the first-class seats where they belonged.

The Nashville train station was packed with cheering friends and family waiting to welcome the singers home. But the celebrations didn't last long. Ten days later, Mr. White told Ella to pack again. They were going back out on the road. Ella was still bone-tired, but she didn't complain. She loved performing more than she hated the travel.

The problem was that Fisk needed yet more help. The old buildings were beyond repair, and nobody wanted to have to beg for space again. This time, the choir would sing to raise money for a permanent home for the Fisk Free Colored School, now known as Fisk University, and its centerpiece, an impressive building that would be called Jubilee Hall.

But the group was falling apart. Phebe's father's dying wish had been for her to stay out of the choir. Eliza Walker dropped out from sheer exhaustion. Greene Evans argued with Mr. White and quit. Ella had only a few days to find more singers and rebuild the choir.

The first person she and Mr. White asked to join was Georgia Gordon, who had fought with White before the first tour. To everyone's relief, she and Mr. White made peace and she became part of the choir again, singing soprano. To replace Eliza they chose Julia Jackson. She was jittery and nervous, but she had a great contralto voice. Julia had been raised by her aunt and uncle, slaves who hired out their time. The slaveholder caught wind that Julia's uncle was planning to escape, so he hastily sold the couple to the slave yard to be auctioned off. Somebody bought her uncle right away. Julia's aunt was about to be sold too, so the next morning Julia got to the slave yard early. She ran a stick along the fence as if she were just playing, until she found a loose slat where her aunt could slip out. Her aunt was never caught. Like so many other Fisk students, Julia had been a teacher, in a school so poor that she had built the students' benches herself.

THE LASH.

The lash was a common form of punishment.

Bass singer Edmund Watkins replaced Greene Evans. He was the only member of the Jubilees to have been a field slave. In Texas, he had had to pick two hundred pounds of cotton every day or be beaten. He managed to escape, but he nearly starved because nobody was willing to hire him. One night, he snuck back to the plantation to see his mother. He was caught, tied to a post, and lashed until his back bled. He ran away again, and this time he found a job, but he was cheated out of his wages. That was when he swore that he'd get an education, so that nobody could ever cheat him again. He enrolled in an AMA college, cooking and washing dishes to pay his way, and soon learned enough to take a teaching job. When the Klan threatened him, he retorted that he'd burn the whole town to the ground if they dared to touch his school.

Mr. White and Ella still needed an alto to take Phebe's place. Mabel Lewis wasn't a Fisk student, but she had heard the Jubilees perform during their first tour. She arrived to meet with them, full of confidence. She explained that her father had been a white Frenchman and her mother a black slave from New Orleans. When her mother's owner's creditors claimed Mabel to settle the owner's debts, he hid her in the home of a general named Lewis. The general took Mabel to New York, sent her to school, and treated her like his own daughter. But when Mabel was ten, the family went off to Europe and left her behind with the servants. The servants were so mean to her that she ran away. She had been on her own ever since, trying to find a place where a girl of mixed race could fit in. Being with the Jubilee Singers was her first experience of living among black people. When she joined, she said, it felt odd "to be with my people. All my life I had lived among white people and was punished if I were seen talking with colored people."

Over the next months they sang in dozens of cities, from Chicago, where buildings were still charred from the great fire, to Boston, where they sang in a giant coliseum to an enthusiastic audience at the World's Peace Jubilee. Though the second tour was exhausting, fame made it easier. The American Missionary Association gave them staff, so that all the planning didn't fall on George White's shoulders. They rode for half-fare on trains that had earlier refused to give them seats. They didn't have to sing on street corners to attract an audience; every concert was sold out as soon as it was announced. Ella wrote, "Success is now at hand. Our concerts are so well attended that many are doomed to stand and many more leave for want of room. In some cities excursion trains are going to run to the places where we sing."

They sang to thousands at the great coliseum for the
World's Peace Jubilee in Boston.

The Jubilee Singers came to realize that fame gave them power, and they began to use that power. In Baltimore, they heard that blacks couldn't buy tickets to their concert. One of the singers (reports are mixed about whether it was Isaac, Ben, or Tom) went to buy a ticket and found out that the rumor was true: the ticket seller didn't recognize him and wouldn't sell him a ticket because he was black. From then on, they refused to sing to segregated audiences.

Their fame did not persuade everyone. In Elizabeth, New Jersey, they had no trouble booking rooms in a boarding house, but when they arrived it was deserted. The staff had walked out when they learned that they would be serving black people. Eventually the landlord appeared and showed them to their rooms himself. It was a Sunday night and no concert was scheduled, so Mabel asked if they could play the piano in the parlor. The landlord shrugged. "Be my guest."

They stood around Ella at the piano and had just begun to sing when, suddenly, somebody shrieked. They rushed into the hall. On the landing above them, the landlord was struggling to tie up his wife with a length of clothesline. She was screeching that she didn't want black fingers pawing her piano. The next morning the landlord apologized and told them that they could stay in his establishment any time they wanted, but they never took him up on his offer.

After a sold-out concert in New York City, a distinguished-looking man with a neat black beard was waiting for them backstage. The singers strained to understand what he was saying. Ella wondered if he was even speaking English. They'd never heard such a thick Scottish burr.

George MacDonald

The man was George MacDonald. He was in New York with his wife and eleven children on a speaking tour as the celebrated author of *The Princess and the Goblin* and many other fairy tales and fantasy novels. (Today he is best remembered for inspiring the author of *The Lord of the Rings*, J. R. R. Tolkien, and the man who created the world of Narnia, C. S. Lewis.) MacDonald's whole family had come to hear the Jubilees, and they were so impressed that MacDonald invited them to tour England. They would sail across the ocean that their great-grandparents had crossed. This time, there would be no shackles and chains.

THERE'S A MEETING HERE TONIGHT

CHORUS
Get you ready, there's a meeting here tonight,
Come along, there's a meeting here tonight;
I know you by your daily walk,
There's a meeting here tonight.

FIRST VERSE
Camp-meeting down in the wilderness,
There's a meeting here tonight.
I know it's among the Methodists.
There's a meeting here tonight....

"There's a Meeting Here Tonight" is one of the exuberant spirituals from the Revival movement. Revivals were large religious gatherings where preachers promised that, even if people were facing hardships, they could look forward to a better life in heaven. Many abolitionists, white and black, were part of the Revival movement. Despite their message of hope and joy, the meetings were segregated. Revivals still take place, and the attendees often sing "There's a Meeting Here Tonight." Conveniently, the reference to Methodists is easy to change, depending on the denomination involved.

Chapter 8

BREAKING THE CHAINS

"[Do not] wink at this thing now that we are free. We should exert ourselves in breaking the chains of those who are still in bonds."
—*Jubilee singer Benjamin Holmes, at a performance for Britain's Anti-Slavery Society*

"May I have the names of the passengers, sir?"

The young man at the steamship office's ticket booth took the list that George White handed him. He counted the names twice, wrote down a sum with a stub of pencil, scratched it out, added it up again, and handed White the bill. For once, White didn't flinch. The Jubilees had the money to sail to England in comfortable cabins. He tapped his pockets, looking for his billfold. "Aha! Found it." He began to count out the cash.

"I hope the accommodations will be to your liking," said the young man.

"I know the Jubilee Singers will be well pleased."

"The Jubilee Singers?" The clerk looked away. "I'm afraid we cannot accommodate you after all, sir," he muttered.

White tried to stay calm. "May I ask why not?"

"I am an admirer of your Jubilee Singers, but I'm afraid we cannot provide for their comfort after all. I am sure you understand. May I help the next customer, please?"

White stepped out of the line. In his pocket, he had letters of recommendation from Mark Twain and Henry Ward Beecher. Surely they counted for something? He soon learned that the letters didn't count for much with American steam-ship companies. He couldn't get cabins on any of their ships.

Desperate, he tried a British company and almost cried with relief when he had the tickets in his hand. On a sunny April day in 1873, the Jubilee Singers walked up the gangway of the massive steamship *Batavia*. They were as giddy as little children.

Mr. White herded everybody into the grand saloon before the ship even left the New York dock. "Attention, attention, Jubes!" he cried, waving a manual of rules over his head.

Over the din of hundreds of jostling passengers popping champagne corks, he read out instructions about what to wear, warnings about eating too much, and the rules of shipboard etiquette. When he looked up, only Ella was still there. The others had left to join the raucous farewell party on deck. He shrugged at her and closed the manual. "Most of you were house servants at one time or another," he said. "You probably know more about oyster forks and finger bowls than anybody else on the ship." Together they climbed the stairs to the deck to take a last look at New York.

The singers shared staterooms on the steamship *Batavia*.

The ocean heaved and fell, and made the singers so seasick that they couldn't get out of their berths for the first few days. When they finally got used to the thrumming of the steam engine, they ventured on deck to breathe the fresh, salty air. Maggie Porter remembered, "I can see the young girls of the company now as they must have looked to our fellow passengers, each one wearing a calico wrapper with head bound up in long woolen scarfs, creeping cautiously to her deck chair prepared to be sick.... Five long days I was ill. At last I got my sea legs, and with it a sea appetite, to which I did justice five times a day."

Britain had a complex history in regard to slavery. The nation had once been a brutal player in the "peculiar institution," when the slave trade into the West Indies was making it fantastically rich. There was enormous money to be made from crops like sugar and cotton, and it was cheaper to work slaves to death and replace them than to treat them well. It is estimated that from 1690 to 1820, some 748,000 slaves were sold to Jamaica alone.

At the same time, Britain had a strong abolitionist tradition. Black activists, ministers of various religions, and thousands of other citizens gave presentations at Parliament, marched in protest, circulated petitions, and did whatever they could to stop the trade in human beings. Though British women didn't have the vote, many used what influence they had in the fight against slavery. For example, women controlled most households, so when many decided to boycott slave-produced sugar, three hundred thousand families found non-slave sources of sugar or drank their tea without it.

Britain had abolished the slave trade in 1807 and banned slavery in its colonies in 1833, but during the Civil War many British sympathized with the South, partly because they were

The Jubilee Singers gave their first London concert at the city's most imposing venue, Willis's Rooms.

still hungry customers for cotton and other slave-produced goods. Now that the slaves had been freed, how welcome would a black choir be?

The Jubilee Singers' first London concert was to take place at a gorgeous venue called Willis's Rooms. They dressed in the finest clothes they had ever owned: tailored suits and snowy white shirtfronts for the men, and silk dresses with high collars and touches of lace for the women. One of the most respected people in all of England, the Earl of Shaftesbury, was going to

Lord Shaftesbury preached against many social ills.
He worked tirelessly to end slavery.

introduce them. Old Lord Shaftesbury had been born to every
privilege, and he had used his vast wealth and influence to do
a great deal of good for the poor and the mentally ill. He had
also been a strong abolitionist.

Willis's Rooms was the most lavish place the Jubes had
ever seen. Sparkling chandeliers hung from the high ceiling. A
broad staircase led down to a ballroom lined with mirrors and
great oil paintings. At the first opportunity, Ella played a few
fast scales to get the feel of the grand piano.

Moments later, the ornate doors opened wide. May was
the month when England's high society came to London for
parties, and on May 6, 1873, every member of the nobility

seemed to have come to hear the Jubilee Singers. Six hundred titled ladies and gentlemen, dressed in elaborate silks, sat facing the nervous choir.

The audience clapped politely. One or two ladies giggled behind gloved hands. Ben stood up on behalf of the Jubilees and made a quick bow.

Lord Shaftesbury was helped onto the stage, but his introduction was not impressive. After telling the lords and ladies that the choir would sing "the old slave songs composed by their fathers in the darkest hours of their bondage," he added that they shouldn't expect much artistry. Would London be like New York? Would the choir be insulted and told that their songs were not "real music"?

The Jubes took their places around Ella at the piano. They stood as close to each other as they could, so they could hear one another's voices. Ella lifted a finger and they sang the first sweet note of "Steal Away."

The privileged, powerful men and women seated on their gilt chairs had never heard spirituals before. They couldn't have had less in common with this choir of young Americans who had been slaves for half their lives. But all the walls that divide people—race, geography, wealth, history—fell away to the cry, "I ain't got long to stay here." By the time the last note melted away, the audience was weeping.

After the concert, the fine ladies and gentlemen forgot about decorum and shoved their way to the stage. A lady grabbed Ella's hand and said, "If the way you sing is not the highest artistry, I do not know what is."

Two of the highest-ranking people in the glittering audience were the Duke and Duchess of Argyll. When Lord Shaftesbury introduced them to the singers, they invited the troupe to perform for a small entertainment they were planning at their home the next afternoon.

A servant sent George White a printed list of etiquette rules. All the next morning, the Jubes tested one another on how to act in the presence of nobility. They spent so much time practicing how to curtsy and bow that when the duke's carriages came for them, they had to scramble to get ready.

Rain drummed against the cobblestones as the carriages arrived at Argyll House. As the singers clambered down from the carriages, servants were waiting to take their wet cloaks. Another servant led them to the drawing room, through a small paneled hallway where fragrant rosemary was burning in a bowl to scent the air.

After welcoming them, the duke was full of questions about their lives as slaves. Benjamin was just describing what it felt like to be locked into a slave pen when a servant handed the duke a small card on a silver tray. The duke excused himself at once. They saw him escort two newcomers—a short middle-aged woman and a much younger one—past the guests and into another drawing room. Mr. White looked as if he was about to faint. What was going on? Ella described the scene:

> A messenger beckoned us to follow him. We were led in haste into a spacious drawing room, elegantly furnished, and left alone for a few moments. We quietly stood gazing upon the exquisite objects all about us, occasionally exchanging a nod or whisper of admiration, until we discovered at the other end of the room, some distance off, a stout, ruddy-faced lady sitting, simply dressed in black, and at her feet sat a young girl simply attired. We bowed slightly as we would to any stranger, and became silent, thinking it odd that they should sit in the middle of

Victoria, Queen of the United Kingdom of Great Britain and Ireland.

the room. A moment later ... the Duke of Argyll entered, looking as though he wondered that the floor had not swallowed us; but before we could realize the cause, he had advanced, and bowing extremely low, addressed the lady as "Your Majesty"! and began introducing us. Some of us, at least, had always thought of Queen Victory [sic] as young and beautiful, clothed in royal robes, crowned, and with scepter in hand. That matronly looking lady, dressed like ordinary mortals, Queen Victoria! contradicted our conception of a queen. Our faces must have reflected something of this astonishment, and a sense of the ludicrous must have struck Her Majesty and us simultaneously, for ripple after ripple flitted across her flushed motherly face and ours, and she and we, for a moment, were convulsed with laughter.

In a deep voice the queen addressed the duke: "It is my pleasure that they sing 'Steal Away.'"

As they sang, the Jubes kept their eyes on the wall over Victoria's head to avoid making the mistake of staring straight at the queen. After "Steal Away," they sang "The Lord's Prayer."

The queen didn't clap when they finished. Instead, she spoke to the duke: "Tell them we are delighted with their songs, and that we wish them to sing 'Go Down, Moses.'"

The queen's teenage daughter, Princess Beatrice, dabbed her eyes while they sang, but the queen's expression didn't change. When the concert was over, the Jubilees stood in silence until Queen Victoria—that small widow who was the sovereign of so many lands—had left the room.

Barely ten years had passed since Edmund Watkins had been tied to a whipping post and lashed, Ben Holmes had been behind bars in a slave yard, and Jennie Jackson had scrubbed

Benjamin Holmes was imprisoned in a slave pen like this one when he learned that slaves had been set free.

other people's dirty clothes until her knuckles were raw. It was less than ten years since Ella had had to sneak up the back stairs of her music teacher's house in the dark of night. Now, royal approval opened every door to the Jubilee Singers. Requests to give concerts poured in. Almost overnight, books appeared about their former lives as slaves. At every concert, copies of their songbooks and signed photographs sold out. Newspapers followed their every move.

Fans showered them with notes and gifts. Women swooned over Tom and Isaac, sending them steamy love notes. Everywhere the singers went, people asked them about the range of their skin color, from pale Mabel to ebony-black Tom,

Maggie and Isaac pose with fans. Fans followed the singers everywhere they went, even trying to touch their dark skin.

One of Britain's strongest abolitionists was Josiah Wedgwood, the manufacturer of fine china. Wedgwood made this porcelain anti-slavery medallion showing a kneeling slave and the inscription "Am I not a man and a brother?" Aristocrats wore the medallions to show their support.

Jennie, and Maggie. They were especially fascinated by Jennie and Maggie, and would often ask if they could touch them.

The Jubes enjoyed the attention, up to a point. They realized that part of the admiration was plain curiosity, just as it had been at their very first concert. Victorians loved what they called *curiosities*—this was an age when people came home from their travels with exotic plants and keepsakes, and some questionable finds like a mermaid's hand—and they considered these former slaves to be very exotic indeed. On top of everything else, they were descendants of Africans.

The British public's fascination with all things African had been fired up by daily reports about the explorer David Livingstone. Livingstone, a doctor and missionary, was also a great explorer of Africa. He crossed the continent several times, charting many bodies of water that Europeans hadn't known about, including Victoria Falls. He had also been a horrified eyewitness to the African slave trade and had fought hard to abolish it. When he disappeared and a well-known journalist went looking for him, the news stories about Africa held readers spellbound. Many of the stories were completely bogus, if not downright idiotic, but readers didn't seem to care. Africans might as well have been Martians, for all the nonsense talked about them.

When people asked ridiculous questions, it helped to have a sense of humor. Mabel Lewis wrote about a woman who confided to a friend, while approaching them as they were waiting at a station, "'I am going to speak to some of them and see if they speak English.' She came up to me and said, 'Do you speak English?'

"'Ugh?' I said.

"'Do you speak English or do you just learn the songs?'

"'Baca migly pan martu,' I answered.

"And she said, 'I guess they do not talk, they only sing in English.'"

Mabel thought the encounter was hilarious.

The Jubilee Singers were caught up in a whirlwind that took them all over England and on to Scotland, Wales, and Ireland. They gave private concerts in the homes of aristocrats, sold-out public concerts, and free performances at orphanages and anti-alcohol meetings. They met with the very rich; Prime Minister William Gladstone and his wife invited them for breakfast. And they met the very poor. In Edinburgh, Ella was in tears when they sang at a breakfast for seven or eight hundred of the city's most impoverished people.

Their last concert in England brought in more money than they had ever made before. Ben Holmes summed it up: "The foundation of Jubilee Hall, which was laid last spring with American greenbacks, will be capped with British gold."

When the singers left England to sail home in triumph, Lord Shaftesbury was on hand to tell them goodbye.

GO DOWN, MOSES

When Israel was in Egypt's land: Let my people go,
Oppressed so hard they could not stand, Let my People go.
Go down, Moses,
Way down in Egypt's land,
Tell old Pharaoh,
Let my people go.

"Go Down, Moses," as it appears in the Jubilees' own song-book, has twenty-five verses. On the surface it refers to Moses leading the Hebrews out of slavery in Egypt, a Bible story that meant a lot to slaves. It is also associated with Harriet Tubman, who was called Moses because she led so many to freedom.

Chapter 9

THE GOOD WE MIGHT DO

"How much good we might do not only for others
but for our own people and hearts!"
—*Ella Sheppard's last entry in her diary*

W hen they were all settled with teacups balanced on their knees, Mr. White cleared his throat. "George," he said, "won't you tell Ella how it is that you are studying at Fisk?"

George Moore didn't need prodding. "My father was a slave who was taught to be a tinsmith. My mother was white, as you can tell by my hue, but she was kidnapped when she was a girl and sold into slavery. My father managed to escape, but before we could follow, my mother and I were sold. I won't trouble you with all we experienced, none of it good. My father somehow found us and brought us up to Nashville. He set up a tin shop in a stable in an alley—we made most of the pails and gutters and garbage cans you use to this day at Fisk. As for me, all I wanted to do was play with my friends in Smoky Row. I thought books were boring, and I sure wasn't interested in school. But my father was determined to change my mind. Can you guess how he succeeded?"

George paused for effect. Ella couldn't take her eyes off him.

"He said, 'Let's go for a walk, son.' He took some of his tools and thirty cents and we set off over the same ground he'd covered when he was a fugitive. He had me drink from the same streams, he showed me where he had hidden by day, and he pointed out the houses where people had given him a crust of bread or a slice of pie. We kept body and soul together by fixing

George Moore

roofs and buckets along the way. I reckon we must have walked three thousand miles. By the time we got back to Nashville, I'd seen enough to know that I needed an education."

Right there and then, Ella decided that one day she would marry George Moore.

The Jubilee Singers arrived home in the spring of 1874. They had earned $50,000 for Fisk during their brilliant tour of Britain, but their success came at a terrible price. Minnie's and Mabel's voices were in tatters. Benjamin had a cough he couldn't shake. George White's wife, Laura, had died of typhoid fever in Glasgow. The sorrow broke him; he was so ill from exhaustion and grief that Ella had to buy a mattress so that he could be carried onto the ship.

Despite all this, the trip to England had been an amazing experience, allowing them the respect and admiration they deserved. Better yet, for the first time in their lives they had been treated as equals, or at least cordially, wherever they went. Now they were back in a United States where the lines of racial hatred were hardening into stone.

In 1875, the U.S. Congress passed the Civil Rights Act. Though blacks and whites couldn't go to public baths together or drink in saloons together or even get their hair cut in the same places, under the Civil Rights Act, other rights were now defined by law. Schools, trains, churches, hotels, and even cemeteries had to serve people of any color. Blacks could even sit on

Queen Victoria was such an admirer of the Jubilees that her own court painter, Edmund Havel, painted the Jubilee Singers in 1873. From left to right, the men are Benjamin Holmes, Isaac Dickerson, Thomas Rutling, and Edmund Watkins. From left to right, the women are Mabel Lewis, Minnie Tate, Ella Sheppard, Jennie Jackson, Julia Jackson, Maggie Porter, and Georgia Gordon.

juries. The Freedmen's Bureau shut down. The northern troops that had protected black schools were gone.

The law was one thing, however, and attitudes were another. Instead of ensuring peace, the Civil Rights Act ignited a firestorm. Hatred didn't have to hide under the hoods of the Klan anymore. Newspaper headlines warned white people to band together to save themselves from the supposed "Black Threat."

A black candidate who dared to run for office in Tennessee was murdered. A seventeen-year-old black schoolteacher, Julie Hayden, was murdered. The streets were so dangerous that Fisk's students could not go out at night. Twenty-seven thousand black people left Nashville for the northern states, where they hoped they could live in peace.

Most American states, especially in the South and Mid-west, passed local laws named after Jim Crow, that black character in minstrel shows. These laws took away most of what the Civil Rights Act had granted. The most common Jim Crow laws were against intermarriage, but there were many more. Bus and train stations had to have separate waiting rooms and separate ticket booths for white and black passengers. White nurses did not have to take care of black patients. Black barbers couldn't touch the hair of white women or girls. Any employer who had white and black staff had to make sure they had separate toilets. Schools for white children and black children had

GRIP.   SATURDAY, 1ST OCTOBER, 1881.

THE COLOUR LINE.

The "Queen's" Man.—Queen's Hotel, sir! Come right along with me, sir! Queen's Hotel, first buss—leading hotel in the city for white men—give us your checks, sir!

In Toronto in 1881, a newspaper ran a cartoon of the manager of the Queen's Hotel—a fictional stand-in for the Continental Hotel—welcoming a seedy white man. The Jubilees, who had been barred from the hotel, look on in the background. When whites heard, many opened their homes to the Jubilees.

A café in Durham, North Carolina, had separate entrances for its customers.

to be separate, and they couldn't even share textbooks. Libraries were segregated. Blacks and whites couldn't be housed together in mental hospitals or even in reform schools. Even blind people were not allowed to be served in the same facilities. In Georgia, it was unlawful for any amateur white baseball team to play on a diamond or even on a vacant lot if it was within two blocks of a playground for blacks, and vice versa. Even local fishing spots were segregated. And in the State of Mississippi, a person could be fined five hundred dollars or jailed for six months just for spreading printed, typed, or written matter that argued for equality.

In 1896, the Supreme Court said that having separate railway cars for blacks and whites was legal as long as those railway cars were equal. This "separate but equal" rule was applied to all kinds of facilities, and it was allowed until 1954, when the Supreme Court ruled that schools could no longer be separate. Even then, it took years to enforce the new laws.

Some schools stayed segregated until 1968. The fight for equal rights had just begun.

Now that they were home, the Jubilee Singers spoke out courageously against Jim Crow laws wherever they could. They refused to perform to segregated audiences and, unless there was no other choice, they refused to stay in segregated hotels. Most of the Jubes refused to give concerts in the South. Whenever she could, Ella Sheppard gave speeches to women's clubs, church groups, and politicians about the evils of segregation.

After many years on the road, Ella longed to have family around her. She went to Okolona, Mississippi, and found her mother, Sarah, and her half-sister, Rosa, in their log-cabin home. She brought them back to Nashville and built a house for them near Fisk. She paid Rosa's tuition to Fisk so that the girl could become a teacher. Ella also remained close to her stepmother, Cornelia. She supported her, as well as Sarah and Rosa. And she became engaged to the handsome George Moore.

In January 1875, the Jubilee Singers were invited overseas again, this time to Europe. They were only too happy to leave the United States and its Jim Crow laws behind, for even a few months. Once again, Ella and George White quickly rebuilt the choir. Only Tom, Maggie, and Jennie were left from the original troupe.

The Jubilee Singers gave countless public concerts all over continental Europe. They performed for royalty in Holland and Germany and Switzerland, in palaces so luxurious that, in one, even the butler wore diamond studs in his shirt. It didn't make any difference that their audiences couldn't understand the English words. They didn't have to. The music spoke its own language. In Amsterdam, Ella wrote, "Our arrival created a greater sensation than a circus in the United States. We could not go walking or shopping on foot because crowds of children in wooden shoes surrounded us…."

The tour was turning out to be their biggest success ever, but for Ella the joy was gone. She was homesick for George Moore. Although she was only twenty-four, she was tired and depressed. The singers worked harder than they ever had before; in Germany alone they sang sixty-eight concerts in forty-two

The singers sold poster-like photographs as concert souvenirs. Though the date 1871 appears on the photograph, the image is of singers who joined the Jubilees several years later. On the back of the photograph, Frederick J. Loudin, who joined the singers in 1875, wrote: "Take Notice. Please paste the date of the Concert on the back at the bottom, so as not to soil the front. You will be expected to return all of the photographs to the place where the concert is held on the evening of last concert. [*sic*] Very respectfully yours, F. J. Loudin."

towns in sixty-eight days. Though Ella tried to make sure the audiences didn't notice, behind the scenes the choir was falling apart. The singers weren't eager teenagers anymore. They were grown men and women who had strong opinions about whether a window should be left open or not, who would share rooms, and who was getting the most attention. They expected Ella to settle every squabble. She hated the role, and constant tension headaches left her dizzy. Toward the end of the tour, her hands shook so much that she could hardly use a pen.

On the return voyage, when the Statue of Liberty came into sight, the Jubilees gathered on deck to sing together once more. After the "Battle Hymn of the Republic" and "The Star-Spangled Banner," they chose their last song, "John Brown's Body." By the time they came to the final verse, their faces were wet with tears:

> **Now has come the Jubilee, when all mankind are free.**
> **Glory, glory, Hallelujah,**
> **Glory, glory, Hallelujah,**
> **Glory, glory, Hallelujah,**
> **His soul is marching on.**

A white woman followed Ella to her cabin door. Before Ella could find her key, the woman hugged and kissed her. "I never thought I would or could kiss a negro before! I do thank you. I never felt such music before!" Ella was not one for public displays of affection, but this time she smiled.

That was Ella's last tour, but not the choir's. The Jubilee Singers toured until 1878. Over the years, they re-formed with different members, they went on to sing in Australia, New Zealand, and China. Happily, their legacy has been preserved. Today the Fisk Jubilee Singers still sing to standing ovations all over the world.

On a blustery evening in December 1882, Ella married George Moore in the parlor of George White and his second wife. The air was fragrant with the sharp smell of the pine boughs that decorated the mantel. Mr. White toasted them: "I'm not sure anybody's good enough for my Ella, but I have to admit that this Moore fellow comes close."

George and Ella Moore had a happy life together. George became a well-respected minister and a professor. He taught at Howard University and became the first black trustee at Fisk University. The Moores' oldest son, George, became a doctor. Clinton, the younger son, moved to New York, where he opened a cafeteria. Rosa graduated and became a teacher at Fisk. And eventually, Ella fulfilled her oldest dream—Sarah came to live out her last years with Ella and her family.

Ella Sheppard Moore on the steps of her house, across from Fisk University. To the left are Ella's sons, George and Clinton. Her husband, George, and her mother, Sarah Hannah, are on the right.

AFTERWORD

Ella Sheppard Moore came to be one of the most respected black women of her generation. She published many articles about slavery and racial injustice and became a persuasive public speaker. She worked tirelessly for better lives for black people, especially black women. In 1889, she said in a speech, "Have they [women] had a fair chance in the race of life? No. They have met caste prejudice, the ghost of slavery at every step of their journey during these years of freedom. They have been made to feel that they are a separate species of the human family."

Ella never lost her interest in music. She trained and inspired Fisk's student choirs for many years. In 1913, when she was about sixty-two, the Jubilees were singing at the Ryman Auditorium in Nashville. Before they left the stage, they invited Ella to join them. She sang "Swing Low, Sweet Chariot." That was her last stage appearance. She died in June 1914 from complications of appendicitis.

Ella never did graduate from Fisk.

Sarah Sheppard and Phereby Sheppard, slave and slave owner, shared a lifetime of sorrows and joys. When they grew old, they became good friends.

Cornelia Rohelia Sheppard, the stepmother who had loved Ella like a daughter, outlived her. She died in November 1915.

Sarah Sheppard

Greene Evans was elected to the Memphis City Council and then to Tennessee's General Assembly. He worked successfully to get blacks the right to vote and to hold political office in Tennessee. It was an astonishing victory, even if it didn't last long. Decades would pass before blacks got back the rights they'd been granted.

Benjamin Holmes died of tuberculosis at the age of twenty-eight.

Edmund Watkins stayed behind in England in 1874 to study music. He lived in Europe for years and eventually moved back to New York, though he swore he would never set foot in the South again.

Benjamin Holmes

He lived a long life and died an old man in New York.

Thomas Rutling toured with the Jubilee Singers for many years. He discovered that he had a gift for languages and became fluent in French, German, and Italian. He refused to return to the United States and settled in England, where he gave concerts until illness cut short his performing career. He became a music master at a boys' school.

Isaac Dickerson also left the United States, never to return. When the Jubilee Singers were in England, the Reverend Dean Stanley, Dean of Westminster, offered to pay his tuition at Edinburgh University, where Dickerson studied to become a minister.

Georgia Gordon stayed in Nashville, where she married a prominent businessman. She became active in the National

Association of Colored Women and often visited Fisk. She died at the age of fifty-eight.

Julia Jackson was on the Jubilee Singers' second European tour when she suffered a stroke. Though she survived it, she remained an invalid until she died in 1890.

Jennie Jackson married a minister from Knoxville who became the principal of the Colored High School. She kept touring and eventually formed her own troupe, the Jennie Jackson DeHart Jubilee Club. She died in 1910.

Mabel Lewis never enrolled at Fisk. She became deeply religious, married, and settled in Cleveland with her husband. She died in 1935, as witty and sharp as she'd always been.

Maggie Porter stayed with the Jubilees for many years. She was sick of the discrimination on trains and in hotels and restaurants, so she vowed that she would not visit the South again. She made an exception when Fisk asked her to come to Nashville for the sixtieth anniversary of the first tour. She was a much-loved citizen of Detroit until she died in 1942 at the age of eighty-nine.

Maggie Porter

Minnie Tate toured with the Jubilee Singers until 1875, when she returned to Fisk to study. She met her husband, R. A. Hall, singing in a choir and toured with a choir that Maggie Porter organized.

Minnie Tate

George White never regained his health after the first tour, when his first wife, Laura, died. He left his work with freedmen and moved to upstate New York with his second wife, Susan Gilbert. They were so poor that Susan had to take work as a housekeeper. George White died of a stroke at the age of fifty-eight. Ella spoke at his memorial service, and the latest Jubilee choir sang "We Shall Walk through the Valley" and "Steal Away." Georgia Gordon would write that he "was the true and tried friend of the singers, and a staunch friend of the Negro race."

And that is the story of how a handful of young people, most of them teenagers who had known slavery, abuse, heartache, war, hunger, and hatred, set out to save their school and succeeded. They would earn $150,000, or close to $3 million in today's money, during their seven years together. Every year, today's Jubilee Singers gather at the graves of Ella Sheppard and the other members of the original choir buried in Nashville, and sing, linking their past with the future and keeping alive the memory of their courage and resolve.

Jubilee Hall at Fisk University.

TIME LINE

1791, April 21	**Saint Domingue Slave Revolt**
1807, March 25	**Britain passes the Abolition of Slavery Act**
1809, February 12	**Birth of Abraham Lincoln**
1861, April 13	**Attack on Fort Sumter and the start of the Civil War**
1863, January 1	**Emancipation Proclamation**
1865, March 3	**Congress establishes the Freedmen's Bureau**
1865, April 10	**End of the Civil War**
1865, April 15	**Assassination of Lincoln**
1865, December 24	**Founding of the Ku Klux Klan**
1866, January 9	**Founding of the Fisk Free Colored School**
1867, August 22	**Fisk University is created**
1871, October 6	**Jubilee Singers' first U.S. tour**
1871, November 16	**Jubilee Singers perform "Steal Away" in Oberlin**
1872, July 1	**Closure of Freedmen's Bureau**
1873, May 6	**Jubilee Singers' first London engagement**
1875, March 1	**Civil Rights Act passed into law**
1896, May 18	**"Separate but equal" rule passed by Supreme Court**

FURTHER READING

Anderson, Toni P., *Tell Them We are Singing for Jesus: The Original Fisk Jubilee Singers and Christian Reconstruction, 1871–1878*. Macon, Georgia: Mercer University Press, 2010

Gann, Marjorie and Janet Willen, *Five Thousand Years of Slavery*. Toronto: Tundra Books, 2011

Gorrell, Gena K., *North Star to Freedom: The Story of the Underground Railroad*. New York: Delacorte Press, 1997. Originally published in 1996 in Canada by Lester Books.

Marsh, J. B. T., *The Jubilee Singers and Their Songs*. Mineola, New York: Dover Press, 2003. [This is an unabridged republication of *The Story of the Jubilee Singers by J. B. T. Marsh With Supplement containing an account of their six years' tour around the world, and many new songs by F. J. Loudin* published by the Cleveland Printing and Publishing Company in 1892.]

Ward, Andrew, *Dark Midnight When I Rise: The Story of the Jubilee Singers, Who Introduced the World to the Music of Black America*. New York: Farrar, Straus and Giroux, 2000

IMAGE CREDITS

Title page, receipt for "purchase of Negro slave named Moses" (adapted), courtesy E. L. McGlashan Collection of Documents Concerning Slavery in the United States; General Collection, Beinecke Rare Book and Manuscript Library, Yale University. **Title page, bars of music,** © Tobkatrina/Dreamstime.com. **Musical notes used throughout,** © Argus456/Dreamstime.com. **Contents, ticket,** © Ixer/Dreamstime.com. **Contents, sheets of music,** © Jvphoto/ Dreamstime.com. **iv, back cover top,** courtesy Yale Collection of American Literature, Beinecke Rare Book and Manuscript Library. **4,** courtesy Library of Congress, Prints and Photographs: LC-USZ62-41678. **5,** from *Le Magasin Pittoresque,* 1868, © iStockphoto Inc./Grafissimo. **6,** courtesy Library of Congress Prints and Photographs: LC-DIG-pga-01171. **8,** courtesy Randolph Linsly Simpson African-American Collection; Yale Collection of American Literature, Beinecke Rare Book and Manuscript Library. **9,** courtesy Library of Congress Rare Book and Special Collections: LC-USZ62-31864. **10,** courtesy Library of Congress Rare Book and Special Collections: LC-USZ62-38902. **13,** courtesy Library of Congress Prints and Photographs: LC-USZ62-28860. **14,** courtesy Library of Congress Prints and Photographs: LC-DIG-nclc-02002. **15,** courtesy Library of Congress Prints and Photographs: LC-USZC4-2525. **Book cover (as on 17) used throughout,** © Loraliu/Dreamstime.com. **19,** Ms.q.Cab.3.30. Unidentified African-American male without hands. New England Freedmen's Aid Society, ca.1860s, picture #24; courtesy of the Trustees of the Boston Public Library/Rare Books. **21,** courtesy Library of Congress, Printed Ephemera Collection: rbpe 06002200 http://hdl.loc.gov/loc.rbc/rbpe.06002200. **23, back cover middle,** courtesy of Tennessee State Library and Archives (Nashville), Library Collection. **25,** courtesy Library of Congress Prints and Photographs: LC-DIG-pga-01629. **26,** © North Wind Picture Archives/Alamy. **29,** Library of Congress Prints and Photographs: LC-DIG-cwpbh-02531. **33,** courtesy Library of Congress Prints and Photographs: LC-DIG-ppmsca-35361. **35,** © North Wind Picture Archives/Alamy. **36,** courtesy Library of Congress Prints and Photographs: LC-DIG-pga-02797. **38,** courtesy Library of Congress Prints and Photographs: LC-USZ62-37823. **39,** courtesy Library of Congress Prints and Photographs: LC-DIG-ds-05168. **40,** courtesy Library of Congress Prints and Photographs: LC-USZ62-98515. **41,** courtesy Library of Congress Prints and Photographs: LC-USZ62-37861. **42,** courtesy Library of Congress Prints and Photographs: LC-DIG-cwpb-00129. **44,** © North Wind Picture Archives/Alamy. **46,** Fisk University, John Hope and Aurelia E. Franklin Library, Special Collections. **48,** courtesy NARA: NWDNS-111-B-5240. **49,** from Marsh, J. B. T., *The story of the Jubilee Singers : with their songs,* p. 5. Boston: Houghton, Osgood and Co., 1880. **51,** courtesy Library of Congress Prints and Photographs: LC-USZ62-127756. **52,** courtesy Library of Congress Prints and Photographs: LC-USZ62-128619. **55,** courtesy of the American Missionary Association Archives, Amistad Research Center, Tulane University. **56–57,** courtesy of Tennessee State Library and Archives (Nashville), Library Collection. **59, back cover bottom,** courtesy Charlie & Pam Horner's Classic Urban Harmony Archives. **61, 63,** courtesy Yale Collection of American Literature, Beinecke Rare Book and Manuscript Library. **65,** courtesy Library of Congress Rare Book and Special Collections: LC-DIG-ppmsca-02909. **67,** courtesy Library of Congress Prints and Photographs: LC-USZ62-127757. **68,** courtesy General Collection, Beinecke Rare Book and Manuscript Library, Yale University. **69,** courtesy Library of Congress Prints and Photographs: LC-USZC2-1773. **71,** © Niday Picture Library/Alamy. **74,** courtesy of Cornell University Library, Making of America Digital Collection. **77,** from Marsh, J. B. T., *The story of the Jubilee Singers : with their songs,* p. 24. Boston: Houghton, Osgood and Co., 1880. **79,** courtesy Library of Congress Prints and Photographs: LC-USZC4-3936. **81,** courtesy Library of Congress Prints and Photographs: LC-DIG-pga-01815. **82,** © RosaIreneBetancourt 1/Alamy. **84,** Fisk University, John Hope and Aurelia E. Franklin Library, Special Collections. **87,** courtesy Library of Congress Prints and Photographs. LC-USZC4 2990. **89,** © iStockphoto Inc./pushlama. **92,** © Vosts Images/Alamy. **93,** courtesy Library of Congress Prints and Photographs: LC-DIG-pga-05105. **94,** © North Wind Picture Archives/Alamy. **95,** © Ivy Close Images/Alamy. **96,** courtesy Library of Congress Prints and Photographs: HABS NY, 24-BROK,31—3. **97,** © North Wind Picture Archives/Alamy. **98,** © Minneapolis Star Tribune/ZUMA Press, Inc/Alamy. **101,** courtesy Library of Congress Prints and Photographs: LC-DIG-pga-00842. **103,** courtesy Library of Congress Prints and Photographs: LC-USZCN4-253. **105,** courtesy Library of Congress Prints and Photographs: LC-DIG-pga-02283. **106,** courtesy George MacDonald Collection, Beinecke Rare Book and Manuscript Library, Yale University. **109,** courtesy of Cornell University Library, Making of America Digital Collection. **111,** © liszt collection/Alamy. **112,** © Chronicle/Alamy. **115,** courtesy Library of Congress Prints and Photographs: LC-USZ62-14976. **116,** courtesy Library of Congress Prints and Photographs: LC-DIG-ppmsca-34798. **117,** Fisk University, John Hope and Aurelia E. Franklin Library, Special Collections. **118,** © The Trustees of the British Museum/Art Resource, NY. **122,** courtesy of HathiTrust. **123, 124,** Fisk University, John Hope and Aurelia E. Franklin Library, Special Collections. **125,** courtesy Library of Congress Prints and Photographs: LC-DIG-fsa-8a33793. **127,** gift of Mrs. L. Hudson; courtesy the State Library of Victoria. **129,** Fisk University, John Hope and Aurelia E. Franklin Library, Special Collections. **130,** courtesy Library of Congress Prints and Photographs: LC-DIG-ppmsca-11009. **131,** Fisk University, John Hope and Aurelia E. Franklin Library, Special Collections. **132, 133,** courtesy Yale Collection of American Literature, Beinecke Rare Book and Manuscript Library. **134,** courtesy Library of Congress Prints and Photographs: HABS TENN,19-NASH,7A—3; http://www.loc.gov/pictures/item/tn0017.photos.152884p/. **136,** © Csakisti/Dreamstime.com. **138,** courtesy of Tennessee State Library and Archives (Nashville), Library Collection.

ACKNOWLEDGMENTS

Thanks to the staff at Annick Press for believing in this project, to Kathryn Cole for setting me on the path, and especially to Gena K. Gorrell, a superb writer and the editor of editors.

Special thanks to Sandra Booth and to a number of reference librarians and curators who went above and beyond in locating photographs: Chantel Clark, Fisk University; Jane Winton and Sean Casey, Boston Public Library; Christopher Harter, Amistad Research Center. Sincere appreciation also to Charlie & Pam Horner of Classic Urban Harmony LLC, Katie Hearn and Patricia Ocampo at Annick Press, and to Sheryl Shapiro for her beautiful design.

INDEX